Books are to be returned on or before
the last date below.

he
es
ds
st-
e.

as
as
nd
nd

iis
ht
ile
he
nd
he

STUDY SKILLS

FOR THE

INTERNATIONAL BACCALAUREATE

John L. Tomkinson

Anagnosis
Athens, Greece

Anagnosis
Deliyianni 3
151 22 Maroussi
Athens, Greece
Website: www.anagnosis.gr

ISBN 960-88087-7-4

Photoset and printed by:
K. Pletsas - Z. Karadri O.E.
Harilaou Trikoupi 107
Athens
www.typografio.gr

Acknowledgements

My thanks are due to the staff (faculty) of the Moraitis School, Athens, in Greece, for the generosity with which they readily shared with me their collective experience and expertise.

The sole authority for the aims, regulations and syllabae etc. of the International Baccalaureate Organisation is to be found in the publications of the I.B.O.

This publication was prepared for Anagnosis Books, Athens, Greece, by the author, who is solely responsible for its contents. The International Baccalaureate Organisation was not involved in the production of this book, and does not endorse this, or any other, commercially produced works. For the latest information about the various courses and examinations of the International Baccalaureate, please consult the publications of the International Baccalaureate Organisation at www.ibo.org.

"The object of education is to prepare the young to educate themselves throughout their lives."

Robert M. Hutchins

CONTENTS

Studying for the I.B. Diploma

Understanding Grades and Testing

When you leave school to attend a college or university, you will probably wish to attend a competitive institution, that is, one which has many more applicants for places than places to offer. Such universities and colleges use school leaving examinations, such as the I.B. Diploma and term grades, to choose between the many applicants they receive. Therefore the marks and grades awarded in the I.B. Diploma are not like presents at a party, designed to make everyone happy; they have been devised precisely to discriminate between students' performance, so that the most competitive universities will be able to choose the most successful students, the next most competitive universities the next most successful group of students, and so on.

It follows that the higher grades in a school leaving examination should be difficult to achieve. If they were not, the results would fail to discriminate adequately among the applicants, and the competitive universities would need to find some other method to help them choose the students they wish to accept.

For various reasons, some examination systems have suffered from "grade inflation." Over the years, the requirements for a student to be awarded an "A" grade have gradually fallen, so that a much higher percentage of school-leavers are now awarded "A" grades than was the case previously. For this reason, those examinations are now no longer as useful as they were to the admissions officers of the universities. Too many applicants have too many "A" grade passes to enable universities to identify the "best" applicants. So those responsible for admissions have to find other ways of distinguishing the better applicants from the others.

The I.B. Diploma has not suffered from "grade inflation," therefore its higher grades are achieved only by a high level of performance. It is difficult to get a "grade seven." But this is precisely what makes the I.B. useful to university admissions officers, and why students with high grades in the IB Diploma are looked upon very favourably.

This book is designed to help you to:

- study efficiently for the I.B., so that *you* can obtain the best results you can;
- get the most out of your time on the I.B. course;
- help you prepare for later independent study at university. In order for you to be able to do this, there are some things that you should understand about your education, about how to study successfully,and about the I.B. Diploma course in particular.

Understanding Your Education

Students' thinking about what happens to them at school is sometimes dominated by a false model. They think that their school education can adequately be described as follows:

- The teacher communicates "knowledge" to the student.
- The student receives, retains and absorbs it.
- In tests and examinations the student gives back to the teacher, or examiner, the knowledge he/she has received.
- The greater percentage of knowledge returned in this way (the less the student has failed to "pick up", or the less he/she has lost" or forgotten in the meantime) the higher the mark or grade awarded.
- The sole purpose of studying for the I.B. Diploma is to provide you with the means to enter a university or college.

This crude picture of what is going on in schools and examinations is seriously misleading; and any I.B. student who accepts it as an adequate account of his/her education will never attain the highest grades.

Your education is intended to give you much more than a useful piece of paper. It is intended to make you an "educated person." On your various I.B. courses you will learn how to:

- work independently, managing your time appropriately;
- locate, research, synthesise and integrate information;
- read, listen, think, speak and write critically;
- extend your knowledge;
- deepen your understanding;
- question your own assumptions;
- appreciate the limits of your own knowledge and understanding;

- appreciate other cultures, opinions, and worldviews;
- formulate your own reasoned opinions and judgements;
- communicate your ideas effectively in speech and writing.

You will also learn some very important lessons, e.g. that:
- complex problems rarely have simple solutions;
- there are almost always alternative viewpoints, and that some of these *may* be equally valid, and *certainly* must be considered;
- things may not always be what they seem;
- there are more, and more important, things to be learned than can be obtained from teachers and textbooks in school.

Finally, your years on the I.B. Diploma are the last two years of your school life. They should form a period of transition, since at the end of this time most of you will leave home for university or college. You will pass from a stage of close supervision by your parents and teachers to one of comparative independence, when you will have to live and work by yourself, without your parents looking over your shoulder, and without your teachers being in close contact with your parents. During your time on the IB course, you should learn what it takes to cope successfully with that transition.

Self-Education

In order to be on top of what you are doing on the I.B. course and prepare adequately for independent study at university, you will need to take the major responsibility for your own education and progress. You will need to know from your teachers at a very early stage:
- what you will have to study in each of your subjects;
- the skills you will need to acquire;
- how and when you will be examined;
- the criteria by which your work will be evaluated.

> **YOU MUST TAKE RESPONSIBILITY**
> **FOR YOUR OWN EDUCATION**

The Importance of Time Management

At the beginning of your IB course you may think that you have two years in which to achieve the high grades that you wish on the Diploma: but you do not. Each school year is much shorter than a calendar year, and the second year of the I.B. course is even shorter than the first because of the final examinations.

Many obligations fall upon students during this period. In addition to normal homework assignments, class tests and school examinations, you will have to:

- fulfil your CAS requirements;
- deliver a presentation in Theory of Knowledge;
- hand in your Theory of Knowledge essay;
- hand in your extended essay;
- hand in work for internal assessment for each of your six chosen subjects;
- take oral examinations for certain subjects;
- take the final written examinations in all your six subjects.
- make your university or college applications.

Each of the obligations listed above has to be completed by a certain date. The schools have to send in your work to arrive at the I.B. office by a certain date, so that the I.B.O. can send it out to examiners to be marked, and then check the marking, in order to have the results in time for the universities to consider your applications. If you fail to hand in your work by the dates due, you will forfeit your I.B. diploma.

I.B. DEADLINES <u>MUST</u> BE MET

Deadlines tend to crowd in during the second year, when you should be focusing attention on revision for your final examinations. It is very important, therefore, that you anticipate deadlines so that you do not have to do too much at once. If you do the work too early, it will not benefit from the insights and experience that you acquire on the course. If you do it too late, you will not have time to do it well, and you will become stressed.

Your school may help you spread things out appropriately by laying down their own deadlines. These are for your benefit, and should be scrupulously respected. In the last resort it is your responsibility to see that you have fulfilled your obligations by the due dates.

Success and Failure in School

Detecting The Marks of Failure

Have you ever found yourself thinking any of the following:

- In class I usually doodle, look out of the window, or daydream.
- I can't express myself clearly in class, so I never say anything.
- I don't know how to pick out what is important in what I am reading. I often find myself getting lost in the details.
- When I get to the end of a passage I have been reading, I often cannot even remember what it was about.
- I can't seem to organise my thoughts on paper.
- When I make notes I don't put the right points into them.
- I don't review my notes periodically.
- I don't study enough. I intend to, but I never get around to it.
- I can't study for long periods without becoming distracted and tired.
- I do study, but in a haphazard and disorganised way.
- I spend too much time studying, so that I don't have time for any hobbies or social life.
- When I get written assignments, I just can't get started.
- I usually do all my assignments the night before they are due to be handed in.
- When I revise I find myself daydreaming.
- I can never remember what I have revised, even when I have only just put the book down.
- I usually revise a lot on the night before an examination.
- When I see the examination paper, my mind goes blank.
- I never seem to have enough time in examinations.
- I seem to get low marks on essays, tests and examinations, even when I think I knew the material well and think that I wrote well; and I don't know why this happens.

If you could have made several of these statements, then it is likely that your performance at school has not been as good as it ought to have been. These are all indications of failure. You will need to change this as soon as possible, so as to get the best grades on the I.B. Diploma you can, and certainly before you go to university or college.

In any school the teachers know that one thing is certain: some students will do very well, some will just manage to succeed, and others will fail. This is how it has always been; and this is how it will always be. The question for you is: which group will you be in?

Playing the Blame Game

The students who are successful are attribute their success to their own intelligence and hard work; and they expect to be congratulated for what they have achieved.

By contrast, the students who fail usually look outside themselves for an explanation of their failure. The school was not very good. The teacher was not very good. The textbook was a poor one. The school building was too old. The examination paper was unfair. The examiner was unfair. The student felt unwell on the day of the examination, and couldn't be expected to do much. The examination room was too hot, or too cold, or too humid, or too draughty, or there was a noise outside during the examination. Then there is always bad luck and the evil eye.

Most of these things do occasionally happen. However, since the many students on a single course will have shared the same school, the same teacher, the same textbooks, the same buildings, the same examiner, the same examination room, the same examination paper, the same examiner and the same weather, and since they will have achieved a wide range of results, then these "explanations" generally do not ring true. Differences in individual performance cannot be explained as due to any common factor, such as the teacher, textbook, building, examiner, examination paper, or the weather on the day of the examination.

The virtues or the faults which produce such different results will usually lie in the students themselves. Some students function as better students than others. That is why some succeed, while others fail. Those differences are precisely what the examinations are designed to detect.

Some people are inclined to see success or failure at school as a consequence of innate ability or intelligence. But most students at school or college, at least up to first degree level, are perfectly capable of succeeding in most of the subjects they take. This is overwhelmingly demonstrated by the large number of people who were failures at school in some particular subject, who later took it up and became very successful at it. Looking back on their experience, such people frequently express surprise at their poor record at school or college, and say: "I can't understand why I couldn't do it then."

The Reasons for Failure

The reason for such past failures is usually not so much that the students who failed *could* not do it, as that they *did* not do it.

Students usually fail because they:
- do not know how to study;
- do not study enough; or
- do not study efficiently.

One way of working out what it is necessary to do to succeed is first of all to consider what you should NOT do. Many students actually sabotage their own studies, sometimes in very obvious ways. They:
- miss lessons or arrive late for lessons;
- fail to review their lessons;
- don't bother to listen to advice from their teachers;
- leave everything to the last minute, and then do it hastily;
- fail to hand in assignments;
- never enter the school library;
- fill up their time with anything other than study;
- fail to anticipate deadlines;
- fail to revise properly for examinations.

Others sabotage their studies unconsciously, and in less obvious ways. It is instructive to consider some examples of how people go wrong, so that we can recognise the signs in ourselves.

Some High Roads to Failure

Student A fails to attend classes regularly through unpunctuality and frequent absences. He arrives late in the morning, starts his vacations before school officially finishes, and to returns after school has started. His parents conspire to help him by providing excuses and cover for him.

He is inattentive in class, where he sits on the back row, hoping to chat with his friends, do his homework, or doze. He frequently hands in assignments late, and sometimes fails to hand them in at all. Those he does were done hastily and carelessly. He revises for examinations only at the last moment, and then has

15

to give up on some subjects entirely in order to have a chance of doing anything at all in the others.

Student A is not working; he is wasting his time a school. This is glaringly obvious, and he probably knows it, even if his parents do not. He lacks motivation: the will to work and succeed.

TO SUCCEED, YOU MUST WANT TO SUCCEED

Student B attends all her classes. At least -- she is physically present in the room when lessons are going on -- but she quickly seems to fall into a state of semi-consciousness and daydreams her way through the school day. She never asks a single question, and never takes part in a class discussion. She hands in all her assignments, which usually contain some of the more obvious points taken from the textbook or handouts, using some of the examples given by the teacher, and in much the same words. She has never been known to express in an essay a single thought or opinion which was not previously provided by the teacher in class, the teacher's notes, or the textbook. She revises for examinations when she is told to do so by her parents, by sitting in her room staring at her textbook or at the teachers' notes for long periods of time. Afterwards, she remembers a little of what she has "learned," and reproduces this on the examination paper. Sometimes this is relevant to the question she is supposed to be answering: more often it is not.

Student B thinks she is working as she should, because she attends all her classes, hands in assignments, revises, and does all the things she thinks students are supposed to do. But she is deceiving herself. She is totally passive. She does nothing for herself at all. She hardly ever thinks, and *certainly* never thinks for herself. She just drifts along passively, hoping that success will just happen to her. It won't.

Being a successful student requires some activity on the part of the student. The teacher can only teach; he cannot do the student's learning for her. No one else can do anyone else's learning for her. This is the single most important thing that any book, parent, or teacher can teach.

TEACHERS CAN TEACH, HELP, AND GUIDE YOU, BUT NO ONE ELSE CAN DO YOUR LEARNING FOR YOU

Student C never misses a class. He is determined to do well. He is constantly asking the teacher questions about his performance, and what he should be doing to do better. He puts great effort into establishing the exact requirements of all assignments. Above all, he wants to know exactly how grades are awarded, so that he can improve his scores. The approach of the examination provokes him into a frenzy. He asks some questions several times. He wants everything repeated over and over again. But what student C never asks about is the subjects he is supposed to be studying. He may say: "If the examiner asks 'Why did Mussolini ally himself with Hitler?' what should I say?" He never asks "Why did Mussolini ally himself with Hitler?" His attention is entirely taken up with grades, and with the outward marks of success; that is, with himself and his own performance.

Student C may be quite successful, but the best grades will always elude him. They go to the best students, to those who are interested in the subject, and not to those who are interested only in improving their grades. It is immersion in the subject which creates real success.

It is important for a student to be self-aware; to be conscious of what he is doing and of what it takes to do it well. This is what this book is designed to help you with. But desire for success in terms of grades, by itself, will never produce real success. Being aware of what it takes to make a good soccer player, will never, by itself, ensure that you become a good soccer player. To do that, you need to play soccer, and to immerse yourself in the game. This is true no less of studying. To do well in French Literature, you must immerse yourself in French literature; to do well in Chemistry, you must immerse yourself in chemistry.

> **BE AWARE OF YOUR PERFORMANCE**
> **AND WHAT YOU NEED TO DO TO SUCCEED**
> **BUT ABOVE ALL**
> **IMMERSE YOURSELF**
> **IN THE SUBJECTS THEMSELVES**

In some ways, student D is very like student C. She is determined to do well. She also constantly asks the teacher questions about what she should be doing, and what the class will be doing next month. She wants to know of each assignment: how many words it should be; how many sheets of paper should be used; whether she should write on both sides; how wide the margins should be; what colours of ink are permissible; and so on. Long before an examination, she wants to know when she should start revising; how many hours a day; what she should revise; whether it should include this topic or that one.

Unfortunately, that is usually as far as it goes. As each question is answered, she moves on to prepare further questions for the teacher to answer. She never does anything with the answers she has received.

Student D probablyworks quite hard – in her own way. She works hard at fussing about peripheral things, without actually spending much time actually studying. This kind of activity is a *substitute* for learning. It is camouflage, contrived by the student in advance to account for anticipated failure. She is probably thinking, "If I have fussed enough enough about everything, then by the fuss I have made I shall have established that I was doing something. Student D is working hard at avoiding work, and working hard at disguising what she is doing, probably even from herself.

> **DON'T FUSS ABOUT PERIPHERAL THINGS**
> **DON'T PREPARE EXCUSES IN ADVANCE**
> **JUST GET DOWN TO IT!**

Student E is rather like student D, except that instead of being a fusser, she is a complainer. Her barrage of complaints will start early and go on and on and on. "Teacher V does not explain things clearly.: Teacher W expects too much of us." "We don't have many notes on X." "The chapter in the book on Y isn't very good." "Z is too difficult a topic to do."

Student E thinks that somewhere in all that complaining she will have alighted upon a good alibi for when the results come out." In other words: "Whatever happens, I have already amassed enough evidence to show that it was not my fault."

Student F is obviously highly intelligent. He always pays close attention to what the teacher is saying, and shows this by perceptive questions and comments. He delights in class discussions, where his contribution is always relevant, original and sparkling. He is an asset to any class, and all his teachers begin with the highest expectations of him. But when it comes to student F actually doing something, he somehow cannot seem to get his act together. His written work is always disappointing. Either it does not turn up on time; or while it shows an acute intellect, it is lacking in any evidence of hard work. "Don't worry," he says, "My final examination grades will be good." In fact they turn out to be as disappointing as everything else he has done.

Student F always has a reason for these things: sickness, a hard-disk crash; a printer breakdown; he is saving himself for next time, etc.

Student F procrastinates. He has trouble getting things done. He doesn't revise early for examinations because he knows that there is plenty of time left. He continues putting it off until the day when he suddenly realises that it is too late. Student E needs to overcome this problem of procrastination, or at least to find ways of getting around it.

IF YOU DON'T START, YOU WILL NEVER FINISH

These short portraits are all crude caricatures, and there is probably a little of each of these in everyone; but there is sometimes a lot of one of them in many of us.

**LEARN YOUR WEAKNESSES,
AND
LEARN HOW TO COMPENSATE FOR THEM**

How to Become a Successful Student

The successful student, by contrast, is the one:

- Who is motivated to succeed;
- Who is aware of what needs to be done to achieve his goals;
- Who actually gets started;
- Who is actively involved in the process of self-education;
- Who becomes interested in the subjects being studied;
- Who has the persistence and self-discipline to carry his efforts through to the end.

Motivation

The secret of being active is motivation. Before you can succeed you must have a genuine desire to achieve your goals. People who drift into their I.B. studies, and are not committed to them, will put in only a small amount of effort. You must know why you are working for your Diploma. There can be many reasons for doing this:

- to be able to continue your education exactly where you wish;
- to get a job -- any job, or a good job, or the particular job you wish to have;
- to gain self-esteem, or the esteem and recognition of others;
- to reward your parents for all that they have done for you;
- simply because you enjoy it.

Awareness

In addition to being well-motivated, you need to be aware of what you must do to succeed. People who have good grades sometimes like to think of themselves as people with special abilities. The truth is that what you need to get high grades and marks are simple skills that can be learned and practised, just like those necessary to learn to swim or drive a car. You must be aware of the various skills you must acquire to become a successful I.B. student. This book will help you do that.

Execution

You must get started. If you never begin you will never finish.

.

Determination

Having begun, it is important to keep going. For this, you need self-discipline. You will have to:

- Give up the expectation of being spoon-fed, of having the teacher somehow painlessly supply your success for you.
- Learn what will be required of you on the I.B. course.
- Get information on your levels and progress in your various subjects from your teachers.
- Set yourself goals to aim for in improvement.
- Practice the various skills required for your courses.
- Keep your efforts sharply focused and constant.

DON'T EXPECT SUCCESS JUST TO HAPPEN TO YOU
IT WON'T
YOU WILL HAVE TO DO IT YOURSELF
NOBODY ELSE CAN DO IT FOR YOU

In the Classroom

For good or ill, the classroom is the heart of your experience of study. You should attend regularly, be punctual, and use the time well.

Two students attend the same lesson. One learns a lot and goes away with a firm understanding of what he is studying. The other is no wiser than when he entered the room. Yet both were taught by the same teacher. Both heard the same words, saw the same drawings on the blackboard, and read the same texts. What was the difference? It may be simply this: one was a good listener, and the other was not.

The bad listeners usually gravitate towards the back row. There they think that they will not be noticed by the teacher. If the teacher asks questions, they may escape being chosen. If they *are* asked a question and cannot answer, it will be less embarrassing, sitting on the back row, because fewer people will witness their predicament. With luck, they can pass the lesson away daydreaming. People who instinctively make for the back row do not usually intend to take an active part in the lesson.

SIMPLY BEING PRESENT IN THE CLASSROOM
IS NOT ENOUGH
**YOUR MIND HAS TO BE THERE,
AS WELL AS YOUR BODY**

If you ask such people why they are not going to take part, they will usually claim to be bored. They do not realise that they are bored precisely because they are not taking part actively in their lessons. Anybody would be bored passively sitting lessons out all day. The way to avoid boredom is to join in and participate. People who join in are rarely bored, and for that reason they become interesting people. People who do not join in are usually bored, and for that reason, they are usually boring people.

How to be a good listener

- Arrive in the classroom with an interest in the material to be covered. The best way to do that is by preparatory reading.
- Focus your attention on the speaker, not your classmates, or on what is going on outside the window.
- Take brief notes. (There is some advice on this below.)
- Listen with an open mind. Don't make up your mind until you have heard everything everyone has to say.
- Listen critically. Think of objections to what the teacher is saying. If you can think of any serious objections, then raise them.
- Don't stop listening when a fellow student starts to say something. It may be useful (or at least, entertaining).

Participation

Participation will make you a more active, and therefore a more efficient, learner.

- The more you speak in class the better at it you will become.
- Think first. You may want to jot your ideas down if you are not very confident.
- Always stick to the point and be relevant. Ask meaningful questions or make relevant comments or observations that relate to the topic under consideration.
- Take the responsibility for your own learning: recognising what you do, and do not, understand. If you do not hear or understand something, then ask. It is quite in order to ask the teacher to:
  - repeat something you could not hear.

- explain something you do not understand.

It is **NOT** appropriate to ask him/her to:

- repeat something you could not at the time be bothered to listen to;
- explain something you made no genuine effort to understand the first time around.

Teachers are coaches, not crutches. They should encourage you, give you hints when you need them, and show you how to solve problems. But they should not do, nor should they be expected to do, the work that you need to do. They are there to help you to learn how to learn for yourself, not to do your learning for you.

> **TEACHERS ARE THERE TO TEACH YOU**
> **NOT TO DO YOUR LEARNING FOR YOU**

Class Discussions

- Speak more slowly than you usually do;
- Speak up, so that everyone will hear you;
- If you realize that you have made a mistake, admit it. Everyone makes mistakes. It is nothing to be ashamed of.
- Concentrate on getting your meaning across; not on how you appear to others or how your voice sounds.
- When you have said what you want to say: just stop.
- Don't get personal. Think about the topic under discussion, not the people who happen to be participating in the discussion.

Lesson Notes

If the lesson is based upon a textbook or notes distributed in class you should supplement the text you have with your own brief notes. If the teacher puts notes on the blackboard, you should take them down and add your own. If the teacher dictates notes, you should also add your own comments and observations to them.

Note taking helps you to:

- focus your attention on the subject;
- understand the subject better;
- provide a basis for your own study and revision notes.

However, never let note-taking become a substitute for thinking and participating at the time. Your primary goal is to understand, not to remember. If you really understand, the remembering will take care of itself.

Progressive Subjects

Some subjects are progressive: you build on one topic in order to understand the next. If you do not understand some basic point at one stage, then you will fail to understand some later topics, and you may not be aware of the reason why. This is particularly true of mathematics and foreign languages. Therefore in such subjects you should not only attend as regularly as possible, you should also ensure that you have mastered any stages which you have missed due to unavoidable absence. Don't forget that daydreaming has the same effect as absence.

Visual Aids

Watching documentaries or movies on the television is not an excuse to switch off. In some subjects, such as drama and history, they may be major means of teaching.
- When appropriate, take brief notes.
- Never interrupt a programme, drowning out what happens next, in order to ask a question. Write your question down and save it for afterwards.

Review

You should go over your experience and your notes from each lesson regularly in order to ensure that what you have been taught has been fully understood and is fixed in your memory. If it has not been understood, you should first try to put things right yourself by going over the book or notes again. If this fails, go back to the teacher.

Coping

There will be times when you may be under great pressure, because you have so much to do in a short time. A good student, especially one who intends to go to a competitive university, will never use these things as an excuse to miss regular lessons. This will only create problems for you when taking the final written examinations.

Developing Efficient
Home Study Habits

What to Study

The time you spend working at school will only be part of the time you will spend working for your I.B. Diploma. Even if you take care to use any study periods at school wisely, you will also need to spend considerable time working at home:

- preparing for and reviewing your daily lessons;
- preparing and writing regular homework assignments;
- preparing and writing assignments in your chosen subjects for internal assessment, your Theory of Knowledge presentation and essay, and your extended essay;
- revising for class tests and examinations.

Many Students work hard yet fail to achieve good results because they work at home inconsistently and inefficiently. They may at times get very enthusiastic, and make a real effort, but they do not keep it up. They may work hard and get tired, yet fail to achieve results because they are not working efficiently. The following suggestions are designed to help you work more consistently and to work more efficiently, at home.

How to Get Started

Sometimes, the time when to study is always "tomorrow" - and "tomorrow" as we all know never comes. This is called procrastination.

Everyone suffers from a tendency to procrastinate at one time or another. It is letting the low-priority tasks get in the way of high-priority ones. It is playing video games or watching a movie on DVD instead of getting that essay completed. It is rather like inertia in physics: a mass at rest tends to stay at rest. For some people this is not a difficult problem, it affects only some areas of their lives. For others, it can be crippling.

When it is a serious problem, the result is wasted time, missed opportunities, poor performance, and consequently low grades.

We can get started on things we want to do, or enjoy doing, very quickly. But, when we see tasks as difficult or inconvenient, it is a very different story. We are very clever at fooling ourselves.

- "I'll wait until I'm in the mood to do it."
- "I've got too many other things to do right now."
- "There's plenty of time to get it done later."
- "I don't even know where to begin."
- "I work better under pressure so I'll leave everything until closer to the submission/examination date."

Then one day, these excuses give way to: "It's too late to do anything about it now."

Once we focus our attention upon them, these excuses don't sound so convincing., but privately, they seem believable.

There are several reasons why people procrastinate:

- Inadequacy: Some people fear, deep down inside, that they are incompetent, and expect to fail. Prevarication is a way of avoiding the unpleasantness of having to put your ability to the test: "If I don't actually do it, I can't make a mess of it."
- Discomfort: Fear of the sheer discomfort of getting the work done is another reason for putting things off. Yet, the more we delay, the worse this problem becomes.
- Perfectionism: Some people think that they have to turn in the best possible paper, and may try to wait until all available resources have been discovered -- which never happens; or endlessly rewrite what they have written, seeking an impossible perfection. You need to recognise that your work will never be perfect, and get on and do the best you can in the time available.

There are several ways to reduce procrastination, or even to avoid it entirely:

- Examine your own excuses rationally and critically, and replace them with positive statements, such as:
  - "There's no time like the present."
  - "The sooner I start, the sooner it will be finished."
  - "It will be less painful if I do it now, rather than wait until it gets worse."
  - "There's no such thing as perfection. If I wait for perfection, it will never get done."

Jumping to the conclusion that you are bound inevitably to fail, or that you are just no good at something, will only create an antipathy to a subject. There are practical steps you can take to put things right.

- **Have Clear Goals**. Think about what you want, and what needs to be done to achieve those goals. Be specific and be realistic.
- **Set Priorities**. List all the things that need to be done in order of their importance.
- **Break Up Big Jobs:** Big projects seem overwhelming. Break them down into smaller and more manageable parts. You'll get more done if you can do it piece by piece. We can all handle jobs we dislike as long as they are for a short time and in small amounts.
- **Get yourself organised.**
  - Create a daily schedule. List the tasks realistically.
  - Have all your materials ready before you begin a task.
  - Commit yourself to doing a task you are dreading. Write a "contract" with yourself and sign it. Make it public. Tell your parents, brothers, sisters or friends what your have decided to do. It will then be more difficult for you to break your commitment.
- Leave written reminders to yourself in conspicuous places: on the refrigerator or on the bathroom mirror. The more you remember what you have to do, the greater the likelihood you will do it.
- **Give yourself little rewards** for success in starting. Self-reinforcement is a powerful inducement to work.
- As a last resort, **Do Nothing.** Force yourself to do absolutely nothing at all -- not even watching the television, listening to the stereo, strumming on your guitar, or talking to anyone, not even daydreaming. Nothing at all. You will soon get so bored that you can begin work on your task.

Where to Study

- Choose somewhere where you are not uncomfortable. Discomfort, such as a very hard chair or an irritating draught, is a distraction. On the other hand, you should not be too comfortable. The idea is that you should work – not go to sleep.
- Ensure that the room is well ventilated. Keep a window open, even if only slightly. Your brain needs oxygen to work properly. If the room gets muggy, you will feel tired, and start to fall asleep.
- Ensure that there is a bright light to read comfortably. The most powerful source of light should be behind you, not in your eyes.

- Avoid studying where there are likely to be distractions, such as loud music, or a refrigerator stocked with food. Needless to say, a television set switched on in the room is not helpful.
- A place where you are used to studying and to doing nothing else is ideal, because after a while, study will seem to you to be the appropriate behaviour in that particular place. As soon as you sit down there you will automatically feel like getting straight down to work.
- If possible, keep your brothers, sisters and friends out. Get used to saying: "No, I'm doing my homework." Practice repeating this to yourself. You can do it. (There are times, however, when visitors can be useful. We will mention those when we come to them.)

When to Study

- Develop the habit of working regularly at the same time each day. If you examine your day carefully, you will find that you tend to do certain things at predictable times. Specific types of behaviour become a habit with us at set times of the day. There may be variations in the pattern from one day to the next, but parts of our behaviour become almost automatic, because they are "time controlled." Such behaviour is easy to maintain once it has become a habit. If you can make studying a habit it will be a lot easier to get down to it.
- Don't break off any unfinished business just before studying. Most people tend to think about jobs they have not finished, arguments they have not concluded or obligations they have still to fulfil, much more than things that they have done and got out of the way. Uncompleted activities and obligations are likely to be a source of distraction to you. Therefore, be careful what you do immediately before you start studying. This will help prevent your concentration from being disturbed.
- Don't do any studying within thirty minutes of a heavy meal. To study efficiently your brain needs a good supply of blood. If your stomach is trying to digest a generous helping of mother's cooking, it will need all the blood supply it can get, and it will take some from the brain. That is why you feel tired and look pale after a heavy meal. If you manage to work at all during this time, you will work so inefficiently that your efforts will be virtually useless, and the time will be wasted.

- Catch yourself when you begin to daydream and go back to your task. But if it happens repeatedly, you are probably tired and need a break. Take it and get it over with, and then you will be able to get down to work again without "drifting."

How to Study

- On each occasion, decide clearly what you are going to do before you start. You must not move backwards and forwards from one thing to another fitfully, without actually getting anything significant done.
- You are most alert when you first sit down to study, so you will be more capable of understanding what you find most difficult. With the worst and most unpleasant subjects out of the way, you won't be tempted to spend long amounts of time on the easy subjects
- Do some work on a substantial task on the day that it is assigned, in order to take advantage of your initial enthusiasm.
- Always set specific goals that you can reach. Don't set a goal as vague and large as. "I am going to spend all day Saturday studying!" That will lead to nothing.
- Before you begin an assignment, write down on a sheet of paper the time you expect to finish.. Keep a record whether you achieve this goal of your goal. It is not much, but it can be extremely effective.
- Some students can easily spend half an hour arranging their books on the desk top, lining up coloured pens, formatting floppy disks, finding paper, etc. They think it is all in aid of getting started, but really it is to avoid getting started. Get yourself organised, and get down to work smoothly and quickly.
- If your mind persistently wanders, don't sit at your desk staring at a book and complaining about your poor will power. If you must daydream, and we all do it, get up and turn around. Just stand by your desk and daydream for a while. The act of standing up helps bring your mind back to the job in hand. You will find that very soon just realising that you will have to get up will be enough to get you back into focus.
- Don't study for a long period at one sitting without a break. The human brain is incapable of concentrating upon a single topic for more than half an hour or so at a time. If you are determined to soldier on without a break, you will find that you are taking one

anyway, because increasingly your mind will wander, and you will have to drag it back to your studies. As time passes, dragging your attention back will become more and more frequently necessary, and get more and more difficult to do. You may end up being able to claim that you have just been reading for an hour, but that you cannot remember anything about what it was you were reading. It is better to take clean breaks for a few minutes, and drink a glass of water or walk the dog. That way you will be able to work efficiently when you do resume your studies -- and you will also have earned the undying gratitude of the dog.

- Frequent repetition is the key to efficient memory work, therefore arrange short but frequent study periods rather than infrequent marathon sessions. Use shorter, more frequently broken up time intervals for review, rote memorisation and self-testing. Allow longer time periods for making notes and writing essays.

- Some slight distraction, such as chewing, helps some people to concentrate. Some music may be fine, but loud rock, especially "heavy metal," will be stupefying. (Some people think it causes brain damage.)

- If you get genuinely tired or very bored, switch tasks, subject, or environment. Stop studying when you are no longer productive. There is no virtue in purposeless suffering.

- Develop ways to be active with what you are studying. Make up a speech and try to teach it to someone else, such as a younger brother or sister – or even the dog, who will probably be more appreciative. Writing, talking, singing and drawing are all active things you can do to make the material your own. Passive reading is not enough.

- Reward yourself for studying, learning a difficult concept, or completing a project. Spend some time with your friends, or do the things you had to put off in order to study. You are more likely to study again and concentrate if you know there is a reward at the end of completing a task.

- Remember: It's not how long you study that counts; it's how efficiently!

WORK SMART: WORK EFFICIENTLY

Reading

Reading is the foundation of the process of learning. Above everything else, a student should be a reader. The most successful students at higher level are the ones who read avidly.

Reading Speed

Because you will have to do a lot of reading, if you are a slow reader, you should try to improve your reading speed.

● Eliminate the habit of pronouncing words silently as you read. Read words without mouthing them, because your brain can read faster than your mouth. You should be able to read most material at least two or three times faster silently than if you mouth the words.

● Read in phrases, rather than individual words, which mean little by themselves.

Types of Reading Matter

It is important to distinguish the various types of reading material you may find in a library. Each will carry a different level of authority, and each will need to be read and used in its own way.

Among the books you may find in a library are the following types:

● The Reference Book: These are not written to be read from beginning to end, but only to be consulted for specific points of information. Encyclopaedias are reference books.

● The Textbook: These are written specifically for use in classes, from primary (elementary) school to university: *Junior Geography; Advanced Level Algebra*. They are designed for use with a teacher and are not intended to stand alone. They sometimes cite sources, though more often do not. They are useful for ordinary essays, and as preparatory background reading ONLY for the extended essay or other research assignments.

- The Popularising Book: These are written by specialists for a general audience, and are designed to make difficult topics intelligible to the general reader. They may have unconvincing titles like *Mathematics for Fun* and *Calculus made Easy*.
- The General Book: written to interest the general reader in a subject which may not be intrinsically difficult, at least to the extent and depth covered in the book.
- The Scholarly Monograph: a book written primarily for academics and students on a single very narrow subject, e.g. *Psycho-Analysis and Women; French Weights and Measures before the Revolution*. They are usually based upon the author's own research. You should rely chiefly upon scholarly monographs for your extended essay and other research papers.

In addition, there may be a periodicals section in a library. Here you may find:

- The Popularising Article: again written for the general reader on an academic topic. These are found in journals such as *Scientific American*, *The Economist,* and *History Today*. The main aim of these is to be clear and entertaining. Articles are usually short, written in non-technical language and geared to any educated audience. They assume no special knowledge, only a general interest, and aim to provide information to a wide audience. They sometimes cite sources, though more often do not.
- The Scholarly Article: Most important in research libraries are the academic journals. These have names like: *Journal of Philosophical Studies, Journal of Theoretical Biology, American Journal of Archaeology, Studies in Philology, Proceedings of the Royal Society of Medicine.*They are published several times a year and sold to colleges and universities world-wide. At the end of each year, that year's copies are usually bound together in a single volume. The articles in them will typically focus upon a very narrow topic e.g. *"The Evolution of Reciprocal Altruism"; "The Sun-King Analogy in Richard II,"* Articles are written by a scholar who has done research. The language of scholarly journals assumes some academic background on the part of the reader. Their purpose of a scholarly journal is to report on original research or experimentation in order to make such information available to the rest of the academic world. Scholarly journals are usually published by universities.

Even if you have access to these, which is unlikely, you will find them difficult. Unless you are a particularly advanced student, they will probably be beyond you at I.B. level. But bear in mind that you will be expected to use them when you are at university.

Assess Your Sources

It is your responsibility to check that the sources you use for your research are reliable. You should never take this for granted. You should always ask the following questions:

- What audience does the author have in mind? Is the publication designed for an academic or a general audience?
- Is the author a recognised authority in his field?
- Is the work up to date or out of date? What counts as out of date depends upon the subject. Some of the political and philosophical arguments used in Plato's *Republic* are relevant to debates which continue to this day; whereas a book on computers dated 1990 may already be seriously out of date.
- Is the author biased in some way? Is he chiefly concerned to gain acceptance for his own political, religious or ethical views?

These different types of reading matter require very different approaches by the reader.

Scanning

The student frequently has to look through large amounts of printed material in order to find what he needs. There is neither time nor necessity to read everything line by line. Instead, it is necessary to be able to cover large amounts of text, learning about their general contents, without having to read every single word. This is called scanning.

Scanning involves the reader moving his eye rapidly over the text noting the key words, which allows him quickly to get the gist of what is being said. These key words are content words -- nouns and verbs – rather than the small grammatical words like prepositions and adverbs.

There is no mystery to scanning. It is not a special skill which you will need to make a special effort to learn. We know how to do it already. It is how we read a newspaper. We run our eyes over the headings of the columns until we find something which looks as if it might be interesting to us, then if it is we run our eyes more slowly over the text underneath. If it proves to be something we really want to read, then we read it properly. You simply apply the same approach to discover what is worth reading properly in all the mass of printed material you are confronted with.

You do not need to read:

- What is irrelevant to your studies;
- What you know already.

When you have found out what is useful, then this material must be read in more depth. But even then, it is likely that most of a book and much of every article, will strictly speaking be irrelevant to your needs. You will need to scan the books and articles you do not reject in order to locate precisely those passages you will need to use.

```
READING TIME IS LIMITED
DON'T WASTE IT
```

Critical Reading

Critical reading requires a much slower and more careful approach. As you read, you should ask yourself such questions as:

- Is there reason to doubt this statement?
- What would support or count against its truth?
- Where did this information come from?
- Could anyone know whether or not this is true?
- Does anyone know whether or not this is true?
- How do they know?
- Is this supposed to be fact, judgement or opinion? (You will do some thinking about these in Theory of Knowledge lessons.)
- Is this evidence relevant?
- Is relevant evidence left out?
- Does the author have anything to lose or gain by what he is claiming?
- Does the author treat the subject fairly and dispassionately?

How to Read a Difficult Book

Sometimes you may have to read a book which is simply very difficult to understand. Look first for the things you can understand and avoid getting bogged down in the difficult passages.

- Study the table of contents to get a general sense of the book's structure.

- Try to establish what the book is saying in a general way by beginning with an overview of the material. Do this by reading the introduction, headings, charts, graphs, diagrams, conclusion, and summary; then take a minute to think about the material before beginning to read in depth.
- Look at the chapters which contain key passages or summary statements in their opening or closing pages.
- Read right on past paragraphs, footnotes, arguments and references that escape you. Concentrate on the material which you can immediately grasp. That may be enough to enable you to understand the gist of the book.
- Alternatively you could try skimming, dipping in here and there reading a paragraph or two, sometimes several pages in a sequence, as you are able. where necessary. You will never get from skimming what reading and study can give you, but you can get a general sense of the contents of a book.

Vocabulary

At the age of four you probably knew about five thousand words; at the age of ten, over thirty thousand. On entering college, your vocabulary will probably be in excess of one hundred thousand words. Words are symbols for ideas. These ideas encapsulate our knowledge, which is stored and transmitted largely through words. Thus when we widen our vocabulary, this is both a reflection of, and a cause of, increased knowledge.

There are some ways which may help you further develop your vocabulary:

- Read and read and read. The more you read, the more words you will come in contact with.
- Become familiar with the glossaries of your textbooks, where technical terms are explained. Use the glossaries, which explain technical terms for you, and make the new terms your own by thinking about them, and by using them as soon as an appropriate opportunity arises. (A sample glossary is printed on the next page.)
- Use newly discovered vocabulary in your assignments and in your everyday communication (writing *and* speaking). Take risks. Without using these new words, they are wasted. You may make mistakes, but it is by making mistakes that we learn. Progress

in many subjects can be measured by the degree to which you assimilate, and make your own, its technical vocabulary.

Below is an example of a glossary, taken from a chapter of *The Enterprise of Knowledge*, a book for Theory of Knowledge (Anagnosis)

Glossary

***ad hoc* explanation:** a purely verbal formula which has the appearance of explaining something but which does not because it was contrived only for that purpose.

animistic thinking: thinking based upon the attribution of consciousness, desires, will, intentions, etc. to inanimate objects.

***a posteriori* knowledge:** knowledge which can be established only through observation.

***a priori* knowledge:** knowledge which is independent of observation.

black box: a model treated only in terms of what enters it or leaves it, without reference to any internal structure or working.

category mistake: a confusion of logical types.

cause: an agency which effects some change.

circumstantial evidence: indirect evidence.

coherent proposition: a proposition such that we know what it would be like for it, and any propositions entailed by it, to be true.

conceptual truth: a truth which is such in virtue of language or logic.

consistency: propositions or beliefs are consistent if they can both be true.

contingent proposition: a proposition such that, if true, they could have been false, and if false, they could have been true.

conventionalism: the view that the hypotheses and laws of science are condensed descriptions of phenomena, without any explanatory value.

data: what is immediately given to the senses.

description: a verbal portrait of something.

dynamic model: a model which represents the processes which operate within a system.

emergence: the appearance of new properties of systems of things not found in their several parts.

Research

"Doing research" means "searching for information." An I.B. student will do research:

- For writing homework essays;
- For the extended essay and for internally assessed assignments in some subjects, e.g. History;
- In order to make good study notes for the final examinations.

The researcher needs sources of information. For this you will chiefly need to use your school library. In addition, your teachers will have information on available libraries in your area. In some countries, however, useful libraries may be few and far between. For this reason, today the Internet is becoming a useful alternative source of research material.

Locating Information

In order to gain the insight and acquire the information necessary to write a good essay or research paper, it is necessary to research the subject. The first problem is to locate suitable source material.

The teacher may give you a reading list. If not, you will be expected to find suitable material for yourself. This may be part of the assignment.

Your main source of information for coursework essays will normally be your school library or other libraries. Your school library will normally be a small one, and you will easily be able to locate the books you need. If you are very fortunate, and your school library is a large one, or if you have access to other large libraries, read the section on using libraries in the chapter on the extended essay.

If you have only a small school library, do not hoard books selfishly. Other people will need them. Try to use them over a single night or weekend. If you have access to the Internet, you may also be able to find relevant and helpful data online.

Reading for Research

The Overview

Unless you already know something about the topic you are writing about, it is generally a good idea to start by reading something elementary, which covers the whole field, so as to get a general overview of the topic.

- Your school textbooks may provide you with an initial and brief overview of the subject.
- In general, encyclopaedias are not acceptable in the bibliographies of research essays, but they may provide good initial starting points for preliminary reading, since they will provide a brief general picture of the topic which will allow you to get your bearings.

These sources will help you understand the broad area of your research and tell you in general terms what is known about your topic. You can use them to get a general background to enable you to "navigate your way around" the subject.

Detailed Reading

In searching for more detailed material, it will be necessary to examine a number of books and articles on the subject. There is not the time to read through this material in the normal fashion, it should be scanned.

Use the contents and indices of books to find material more quickly. The contents page of books written in English is usually found at the front of the book, after the title page, although in some non-English speaking countries it is found at the back. The contents page lists chapter headings. Analytical tables of contents break down the contents of each chapter, section by section, and for that reason, are particularly useful.

The index is found at the back of the book, and lists the appearances of significant topics by pages in alphabetical order. Indices provide details of more specific topics. They are particularly useful if you are looking for references to your topic in books which largely deal with many other subjects than the one you are researching.

Evaluating Source Material

Learning how to estimate rapidly the relevance and authority, and therefore the usefulness, of source material for your research is the most important research skill you should develop.

- Scan the Table of Contents to get an overview of the material.
- Read the chapters that specifically deal with your topic.

As you do, consider the following:

- What type of audience is the author addressing: a specialised or a general audience?
- Is this source too elementary, too technical, too advanced, or just right for your needs?
- Is the material primary or secondary in nature? Primary sources are the raw material of the research process. Secondary sources are based on primary sources. Scholars use primary material on which to found their interpretations, which become secondary sources. You may normally use both primary and secondary sources.
- Does the work add new information to your other sources?
- Does it provide a fresh viewpoint?
- Is it largely fact, reasoned judgement, or opinion? Facts can usually be verified; reasoned judgements are supported by argument and evidence. Mere opinions are of little use to you.
- Does the information appear to be well-researched, or is it questionable and unsupported by adequate evidence? Are any assumptions made reasonable. Note any significant errors or omissions.
- Does it present a review of various viewpoints, or does it view things from a single perspective?
- Is the author's point of view objective and impartial? Is the language free of emotion-rousing words and question-begging terms, showing significant bias? Is it propagandist? Propaganda is the deliberate attempt systematically to determine the interpretation of facts, and is hardest to detect if it echoes our own, or our own society's, prejudices.

Making Research Notes

Skim through your sources, locating the useful material, then make good notes on it, including quotations and information for footnotes. Do it thoroughly. You do not want to have to go back to these sources again.

Ideally, you should make your notes on separate cards or sheets of paper for each author -- identifying them by author.

There are two forms of research notes:

- Bibliographical Notes, which identify your sources;
- Subject Notes, which:
    - summarise points made on the topic you are researching;
    - include quotations you may wish to use;
    - identify other possible sources of information you may wish to follow up.

Bibliographical Notes:

You will need these to:

- cite the sources of the information you employ;
- construct a bibliography listing the works you have used in your research.

If your information comes from a library book, it will be necessary to record:

- The catalogue number of the book in the library
- The author's name
- The title
- The publisher's name
- The place of publication
- The edition
- The date of publication

This information should be obtained from the catalogue or from the book itself.

The catalogue number of the book in the library is needed so that you will be able to find the book again if you need to go back to it to check something, if you discover that you need more information out of it, or if you need to read it again to criticise it. All the other material, except page numbers, is necessary for the bibliography. The page numbers will be necessary to make citations if you use the notes.

The catalogue number of a library book is usually written on the spine. The details required for the bibliography are to be found on the library catalogue cards or on the title page and the imprint pages of the books.

- The title page of a book is the page on which the title of the book and the author's name appear in largest print. The publisher's name and place of publication will usually be found at the foot of that page.

- The imprint page is to be found on the reverse of the title page. On this page is found a history of the publication of the book. This will include the date of first publication.

A book which is quickly sold out in the shops may be reprinted, many times. Each reprint is sometimes called an impression. The dates of the successive reprints or impressions are recorded on the imprint page. Sometimes the publisher decides that the book needs a new look. This may be to update or correct the information contained in it. If this happens, a new edition is said to have been published. The new form is called the second edition. A popular book, in addition to being reprinted many times, may appear in successive editions. Since the text of a new edition may be different from that of the original, and since what appears on one page in the first edition may appear on another page in the second, or not at all, it is necessary to refer to the specific edition which you have used in your bibliography. If no reference is made to an edition on the imprint page, it can be assumed that you are using a first edition, or that there has only been one edition.

The imprint page also bears the name of the printer and the place of printing. This can be ignored. It is the name of the publisher and the date and place of publication which is important, not the details about the printer. Similarly, it is information about editions which is required, not information about reprints.

If the book is a collection of separately written articles in a book or journal, it is necessary to record:
- The catalogue number of the book in the library
- The author of the article
- The title of the article
- The title of the book
- The editor of the book (if there is one)
- The publisher
- The place of publication
- The edition
- The date of publication
- The page numbers of the article

All this information will be required later on.

For an article in a journal, it is necessary to record:
- The author of the article
- The title of the article
- The title of the journal

- The volume number
- The issue number
- The date of publication
- The page numbers of the article

Each year a journal receives a new volume number. The issue number refers to the issues which appear during the year. Thus Vol. IV (3) will refer to the third issue during the fourth year of publication.

Subject Notes

- Make sure that you have understood the author, and that your notes do not distort his meaning.
- Do not merely collect only those things that will support your own viewpoint, ignoring other facts or opinions. You will also need to consider other viewpoints.
- It is absolutely essential, when making notes for an essay or research paper, to make an exact record of the source of each note that you make at the time you make it. You will need these for your references. You may also need to go back to the source of the note for further information or clarification, and you need to know exactly where you found it..

MAKE FULL NOTES
OF ALL THE DETAILS YOU WILL NEED
WHEN YOU ARE IN THE LIBRARY
SO THAT YOU DO NOT HAVE TO RETURN LATER

Researching on the Internet

In some countries, books in English can be difficult to get hold of and expensive to purchase. For those students with access to the Internet there is a patchy but ever-growing source of information available via the computer.

The World Wide Web is a collection of electronic documents which can be sent from one çomputer to another. The system has been given its name because each of the pages on the Web is linked to others by hyperlinks, so that by clicking the mouse button on a highlighted link on one page will cause the reader to be sent another page, possibly on a computer thousands of miles away.

There are three ways of searching for information on the Web:

- If you have Internet addresses of sites of interest, you may go there directly by typing in the name of the web addresses. These Internet addresses, known as URLs (Universal Resource Locators), are typed in your web browser, and on pressing "enter" you will be taken there. However, the Internet is permanently in a state of considerable flux, and web site addresses change frequently.
- You can go to a portal site which is a collection of links to related sites. For example, going to *http://www.anagnosis.gr*, and then clicking on "I.B. Theory of Knowledge" will get you to a portal site with resources on Theory of Knowledge.
- You can use a web search engine which may call up thousands of pages with references to the subject of your research. The largest is Google, at *http://www.google.com*.

Using a web search engine is necessary if you do not know of any sites with material relevant to your research. Even if you do, using a search engine will be useful, since it may reveal the existence of sites unknown to you beforehand.

By entering a word or phrase and simply pressing "enter" you will be given a list of all the web pages known to the search engine which have those words in them. Typically, a search using a search engine will bring a list of many sites, perhaps hundreds of thousands, but many of these will be irrelevant to your requirements. Because of the problem of time lost sifting relevant from irrelevant returns, many search engines provide the opportunity for more sophisticated searches which will avoid this necessity.

- Even the largest keyword indexes do not contain all the information on the Internet, and many tend to specialise in certain types of information. Using A meta search tool is one way of making sure your search is comprehensive. Many meta search tools let you access several data bases at once. These query multiple search engines at the same time from one search query, and then return the results organised in a single sequence.

- Finally, when you do find a relevant page, it will lead you to others dealing with the same subject. By clicking the mouse on the hypertext links (highlighted in blue) on web pages you visit, you will be taken to other (possibly) useful, related sites. This is called "surfing" the Internet.

If you wish to save a page to make notes on it, you may either save in a folder on your hard disk or on a back-up disk or, if you have a printer, you may print it out. It is advisable before you begin downloading material from the Web to create a special directory to receive the files you download, somewhere to put the material you save where it will not get accidentally deleted, and where you can easily find it later.

BEWARE!
SURFING THE WEB CAN BE ADDICTIVE
YOU MAY FIND YOURSELF WASTING VALUABLE TIME
FOLLOWING UP IRRELEVANT LEADS

In many ways the Internet is an inferior source of information than printed matter such as books and magazines:
- It is, in general, less authoritative;
- It is more ephemeral.

For these reasons, most of your sources should be printed matter.

DO NOT RELY TOO MUCH ON THE INTERNET
IF AT ALL POSSIBLE, USE PRINTED SOURCES

Making Notes

Your most precious possessions as a student are your notes. These should be of several kinds:

- Lesson notes: If you are lucky, in some lessons you will be given books of notes or photocopied sheets. Make additional notes on the notes you are given, expanding them as you listen to the teacher. In others, you will have notes dictated, or you will; be expected to take notes as the teacher talks.
- Study Notes: These are the notes you make at home, based upon the lesson notes and your own reading. Making these notes forms the backbone of your private study.
- Research Notes are notes made using the resources of libraries and other sources for a research paper.
- Revision Notes are the brief notes you make of essential points, dates, formulae, etc. in preparation for tests and examinations.

In this section we shall be concerned mainly with study notes.

Lesson Notes

If the lesson is based upon a textbook or notes distributed in class you should supplement the text you have with your own brief notes. If the teacher puts notes on the blackboard, you should take them down and add your own. If the teacher dictates notes, you should also add your own comments and observations to them.

Note taking helps you to:
- focus your attention on the subject;
- understand the subject;
- provide a basis for your own study and revision notes.

However,
- Class notes should be very brief.
- Don't write down details you could get from your textbook.

- Don't be so busy writing that you miss what the teacher is saying. Taking class notes can be counterproductive. In order to retain one point, you miss the others which follow.
- Never let it become a substitute for thinking and participating at the time.
- Use abbreviations.

  NB – note well
  = -- is equal to
  ≠ -- is not equal to
  > – is greater than
  & or + -- and
  V – or
  © – century

Make up your own abbreviations for frequently repeated words.

Study Notes

In addition to the notes you make in classes or lectures, you should be making your own notes.

- Making them involves active reading and thinking about the subject, so that it is the chief means whereby you master the subject and make the material your own;
- It leaves you with a basis for excellent revision notes.

Do not use exercise books. Study notes should be made on loose-leaf paper, and kept in a ring binder, so that additional notes made at a later date may be inserted between others, allowing the order to remain undisturbed. As you read more books, individual pages can be taken out and rewritten, again without disturbing the order.

The study notes you make will be of three kinds:

- Individual points or ideas arranged so as to show the general plan or structure of the topic. (Most of your notes will be like this).
- Direct quotations, formulae, definitions, etc. which must be learned *verbatim*, and which can be used in essays, tests and examinations.
- Original points which have occurred to you, which were provoked by what you have heard or read.

In making notes you should never simply copy (except in the case of quotations, formulae and definitions). Use your own words wherever possible. In addition, you must always understand what you are writing about.

You should try to make your notes:

- Clear
- Comprehensive
- Concise

Reduce information to key points. If you do this, you will have less to remember, and you will have to remember only the important points. Most individual notes will be the summary of a single idea. If you cannot express the essential point of an idea or position clearly and in a few words, you have not properly understood it. They must also, in their arrangement, reproduce the structure or form of the topic. For this reason:

- Use a hierarchy of headings to make clear what the structure of the subject is. Show relative importance of the headings by size, position, underlining or colour.
- Set out your notes numerically or diagrammatically. If they are set out numerically, numbers are used to separate the various points, but also to show the relationship between them, e.g.

  1, 1 (a), 1 (b), 1 (c), 2 . . .

  or   1, 1.1, 1.11, 1.12, 1.13, 1.2, 1.21, 1.22, 2 . . .
- Omit all unnecessary words.
- Use abbreviations. Invent your own.

Make separate notes for:

- Outlines of subjects (main points only – like the contents page of a book)
- Names;
- Dates;
- Definitions;
- Laws and Principles;
- Formulae;
- Lists of various kinds.

These will later become revision notes

The major avenues of cities are lined with neon signs and illuminated advertisements. This is because advertisers know that they have to get our attention to implant their messages into our minds. You have to do the same with your notes. We cannot yet illuminate key words in notes, making them flash on and off, but we can do the next best thing. Make the important things stand out. To do this, use:

The Foundations of Fascism

1. As early as February 1918, Mussolini was advocating the emergence of a dictator: "a man who is ruthless and energetic enough to make a clean sweep." Three months later, he suggested that he himself might be that man.

2. The following year the nucleus of an organisation prepared to support his ambitious idea was formed in Milan. Mussolini called this force the *Fasci di Combattimento*. It was made up of discontented former soldiers who:

    (a) wore black shirts in imitation of
        (i) Garibaldi's red-shirts,
        (ii) the anarchist labourers of the Romagna;
    (b) adopted the salute of the ancient Roman army;
    (c) took as their symbol the *fascinae* of ancient Rome, the bundle of rods and axe which symbolised the state's authority to exercise power;
    (d) wished to be called Mussolini "*Duce*" (from the Latin *Dux* or 'leader').

3. Membership of the blackshirts appealed to:

    (a) discontented ex-soldiers who wished for:
        (i) a sense of purpose, by "saving Italy" as during wartime;
        (ii) some dignity, symbolised by a uniform;
        (iii) excitement;
        (iv) the comradeship of the armed forces;
        (v) respite from the responsibilities and pressures of the family;
    (b) nationalists, who wanted to make Italy great.

4. He was inspired by:

    (a) Garibaldi's "Thousand" redshirts;
    (b) The poet d'Annunzio's seizure of the Italian-speaking port city of Fiume from Yugoslavia. D'Annunzio briefly established a corporate state under his own dictatorship with elaborate uniforms, ritual salutes, and intimidation of opponents.

5. The aims of the *Fasci* were to:

    (a) replace the senate with strong government;

- Capital letters;
- Underlining;
- Bold formatting
- Boxes;
- Highlighter;
- Colour schemes. (Use the more striking colours headings and for the more important points.)

Flowcharts are particularly good for depicting processes, such as solving problems in mathematics, natural processes or experimental procedures. Spider or web diagrams can be constructed to display more complicated relationships.

> ## WHEN YOU HAVE MADE GOOD NOTES
> ## YOU ALREADY UNDERSTAND THE SUBJECT

TWO IMPORTANT WARNINGS

- Do not take your notes to school. As a student, they are your most precious possession. If you carry them around, then one day, you will inevitably lose them. Keep your main files of notes at home. Bring a single file to school for each day's handouts and for any notes you make there, then file them all in their proper places when you get home. In this way:
    - You will carry less around.
    - If you lose your file, it will not be a major disaster.
    - It will be convenient to take the opportunity to review each day's notes as you transfer them.
- Never throw your notes away when the course is finished. You never know when you will take, or even teach, a similar course, perhaps years later. If you do throw them away, you will later regret it.

Opposite page: an example of revision notes (from my *Single-Party States* in the series Studies in *Twentieth Century World History for the International Baccalaureate* (Anagnosis)).

Revision Notes

Revision notes are made in preparation for taking examinations. They have a different purpose from those made in a library for a research paper. They are designed to be an aid to getting material into the memory, and nothing else.

- They must be as short as possible. Each phrase or word is just a hook to call to mind a particular point or piece of information. For this reason, they are best written on small cards.
- The material should be divided into separate points. Only enough words necessary to understand each point should be included. A key word or words, those which sum up the entire point, should be chosen and highlighted.
- Make flash cards for important formulae or names you keep forgetting. These cards with a single point boldly written on them. Carry them around with you so that you can gaze at them at odd times when you have a moment to spare.
- It is very important that revision notes should be so immediately striking so as to grab your attention immediately. Felt tipped coloured pens are the most striking way to give revision notes the striking appearance they need. Two colours should be used, the key words being in a more conspicuous colour than the rest of the notes, so that they stand out even more.
- Because it is easier to understand and retain material that is well-organised, start revision with a good grasp of the main ideas of the topic, then follow with the sub-topics and supporting details.
- Give greater attention to:
  - Points emphasised in the textbook;
  - Areas the teacher has advised for special study;
  - Topics which have come up frequently on past papers
- Test yourself. Write down basic facts and formulae, and then check what you have written from your notes. Don't cheat yourself! Who are you trying to impress anyway?

If you think that you have mastered a topic, could you:

- Explain it to a friend who missed the lessons;
- Apply it to specific situations?

Memory Work

Different Kinds of Memory Work

On the I.B. Diploma course, you will be need to do two very different kinds or types of memory work: general remembering and verbatim memorising.

- **General Memorising** involves remembering the idea without using the exact words of the book or the teacher. You have to remember the substance, not of a set of ideas, not how they are expressed. General memorising is called for in all subjects.

- **Verbatim Memorising** consists of remembering the identical words by which something is expressed. This type of memorising, once universal in all schools but now generally outmoded, is still occasionally be called for in all subjects, but especially in law, drama, science, engineering, mathematics, and foreign languages, where the exact forms of words of formulae, rules, laws, lines in a play, or vocabulary must be remembered.

It is very important for the student to know when to remember the general ideas and when to fix in his mind exact words, numbers, formulae and symbols. It is a good idea to use a special symbol in your textbooks and notes to indicate those passages which need to be memorised *verbatim* instead of being just understood and remembered.

Making memory Work Easier

The following suggestions should help you in your memory work:

- Seek to understand thoroughly what is to be memorised. When something is understood, it is almost completely learned. The very process of trying to understand a complex series of events, or a chain of reasoning, is the best possible process for trying to fix in it mind for later use. That is why, if you have made good notes on a topic, you already know it quite well.

For this reason, it hardly makes sense to try to memorise something you do not understand. What is the point anyway?

> **NEVER TRY TO MEMORISE**
> **WHAT YOU DO NOT UNDERSTAND**

- Try making the ideas clear to a parent, brother, sister or friend without referring to your book or notes. (This is one time when other people can help you study at home.)
- Relearning (i.e. reviewing material over and over again) usually is much easier than learning material for the first time. You save a lot of time over the initial learning. Forgetting is most rapid immediately after learning. You may expect to lose fifty per cent of what you could originally recall within about twenty-four hours. You will probably forget most of it over a week. Thus, if you review a topic before the forgetting process begins, you will be able to review quite rapidly and will have a longer period before rapid forgetting begins to set in again.
- Each time you go back over the material, your memory will improve. If you study a topic only once or twice, even if you do so fairly well, you will soon afterwards forget almost everything.
- If you wait more than one or two days before your review, it will take almost as long to learn it again as if you have never learned it at all.
- If you fail to review notes on a topic you found difficult in class as soon as possible afterwards, your memory loss will make it almost impossible to make sense of it.
- Overlearn. The more you review what is familiar, and so overlearn the material, the easier it is to take a test with confidence and in a relaxed manner. In addition, the more you overlearn something, the longer you will remember it.

It will help to bear in mind that we remember by:

- Association: We pair things, so that recalling one will bring to mind the other. Make associations with the points you wish to remember; the more bizarre the associations, the more likely it is that you will remember them. Make unique, even silly, associations to help you remember.

- Sequences: We associate items in sequences. Make up a story linking the words through the narrative.
- Patterns: We order things according to patterns. Make up rhymes. Rhyming poetry is easily remembered
- Analysis: Reduce the material to be remembered to your own self-made system or series of numbered steps. These can be diagrammed as flowcharts.

Various tricks have traditionally been devised to assist *verbatim* learning by use these facts of human psychology to advantage.

- Representing ideas graphically by use of pictures, diagrams, flowcharts, etc..
- Using memory aids or mnemonics.
  - Acronyms. An acronym is a word or phrase made from the initial letter or letters of each of the successive parts or major parts of a compound term. A popular acronym is "Roy G. Biv" which is used to remember the order of colours of the spectrum (Red, Orange, Yellow, Green, Blue, Indigo, and Violet).
  - Acrostics are phrases in which the first letter of each word or line functions as a cue to help you recall the words that you are trying to remember. A popular example is the phrase "Every good boy deserves favours", used to remember the notes on the musical scale: EGBDF.
- Limit yourself to five or six at any one time. When you read, try to stop after four or five major concepts and review them.

> **BUILD ON STUDY TECHNIQUES YOU HAVE USED SUCCESSFULLY BEFORE. ADOPT NEW ONES WHERE THEY ARE NEEDED**

Personal Learning Styles

People learn in three main ways:
- by seeing (visual learners);
- by hearing (auditory learners);
- by touching, feeling or moving (tactile/kinaesthetic learners).

Ask yourself,
- Do I learn best when I look at something?
- Do I learn best when I listen?

- Do I learn best when I can do things with my hands?

Which are you?

If you learn best when you look at something, you may be a visual learner. If you learn best when you listen, you may be an auditory learner. If you learn best by doing things, you may be a kinaesthetic/ tactile learner. Most likely, there is a little of each of these in you, but there is probably one of these ways that works best for you, while another may be a real area of weakness for you. Discover and employ the approach which best suits you.

Visual Learners: Most people are primarily visual learners. Think of ways to use this strength when you study:

- Read over your material, cover it up and try to visualise it in your mind. Check back, then write or recite it from memory.
- Pay especially close attention to any charts, graphs or diagrams used in textbooks or lessons. Try making up your own, so you have a visual display of the facts.
- Write your notes in a format which is easy to visualise. Use colours, underlining, highlighting, framing, capitalisation, etc.
- Try to create mental pictures of experiments you have witnessed, board work, written materials, etc.
- Make flash cards to learn and to test yourself on formulae, etc.

Auditory Learners: If you are primarily an auditory learner:

- Read your material out aloud whenever possible. Cover it up and try to hear it in your mind. Check back and then recite it aloud.
- Read your notes into a cassette recorder, and then play the tapes back to yourself.
- Explain to a friend the material you are studying, then get him /her to try to explain it back to you.
- Use oral memory tricks where possible, such as rhymes, etc.

Kinaesthetic Learners: Some people are primarily kinaesthetic learners who learn best by doing, touching or moving.

- Write down important points as you read. Recopy them. Write down the important points from memory.
- Take notes during lectures. You will remember what you write.
- Make posters, drawings, charts, etc.

Recognising and understanding your own style will help you succeed on the I.B. Diploma course, because you can learn more, learn more efficiently, and remember better when you use your dominant learning medium.

WRITING ESSAYS

Make the most of class essay assignments. They:
- Make you use your notes and review your work;
- Test your understanding of the material studied;
- Allow you to develop your essay-writing skills;
- Allow you to assess your progress;
- Count towards term/quarter grades;
- Give you practice for the examination.

How to make a Mess of an Essay

It is sometimes easier to approach a problem by considering how NOT to do things. Avoid the following:
- Anonymity. Somebody has to take the blame for writing it.
- No title or question. So which essay is this supposed to be?
- Illegible writing. Somebody actually has to read it.
- Failure to read the question properly and understand it before beginning to answer. (Not a good start. Everything you write may be irrelevant.
- Lack of any obvious plan. Giving a plan as an introduction is a good idea. If you haven't got one you can't give one.
- Ignorance of the basic facts. You *are* supposed to know some.
- Confusion about the facts. You *are* supposed to show that you understand them.
- Introduction of irrelevant material by "dumping" your notes on the general topic. Despite the belief of students everywhere, this is not going to get you any credit. You will be penalised for not being able to distinguish what is relevant from what is not.
- Vague, unsubstantiated generalisations lacking in detailed support. Anybody can make them, so why should anyone give you any marks for them?

- Unnecessary repetition. There are no extra marks for saying the same thing several times; there may even be a penalty for boring the teacher/examiner.
- Failure to control your use of language, so that at times your meaning is unclear. If the teacher/examiner cannot tell what you are trying to say, he cannot give you any credit for it.
- Irrational bias: e.g. "As a communist, Lenin was bound to turn out a murderer. . ." There is no place for this in serious writing.
- Dogmatism: e.g. "Anyone with an ounce of intelligence knows that . . ." This is insulting to the teacher/examiner.
- Moralising: e.g. "If only Hitler had not been so greedy . . ." This is usually irrelevant.

What to Provide in Essays

This varies somewhat from subject to subject, and from level to level, but generally the teacher or examiner will be looking for you to do the following:
- Show that you understand the question and its implications: For this reason it is often a good idea to restate the question in your own words in the introduction.
- Plan your response. Make a plan or outline, either on paper or in your head.
- A complete and well-rounded answer to the question, in which everything you write is relevant as an answer to the question asked. Make no major omissions, and include no irrelevant material.
- Be economical and efficient in your response, so that every word counts, and there is no padding or "waffle".

ANSWER
THE QUESTION,
THE WHOLE QUESTION,
AND
NOTHING BUT THE QUESTION

- Display of a detailed knowledge of the subject, which is entirely relevant to answering the question. Do not show off your knowledge of the subject which is irrelevant to answering the question. Don't "dump" material on the same subject, simply because it is on the same subject, if it does not contribute to answering the question.

DON'T "DUMP" YOUR NOTES

- Provide evidence for all claims that you make.
- Distinguish between facts and theories. This is not always easy; if this is the case, not, say so.
- Display evidence of wide reading, and an ability to employ the results of this work effectively in the essay. Refer, quote, show off a bit!
- Provide a balanced discussion of the issues. Consider all significant points of view.
- Make evident your awareness of the limitations of your claims. Use words like "probably" and "arguably" where appropriate.
- Present your essay legibly and clearly.
- Ensure that it is free from significant numbers of errors of spelling, grammar, syntax and punctuation.
- Adopt an appropriate style.
- Adopt a lively and confident style.
- Elegance of expression. Polish it as you do it.
- Try to be original. Every teacher dreams of one day coming across a student who really thinks for himself.
- Show some sign that you enjoy studying the subject. Don't do anything special about this. If you have enjoyed the subject, it will show up by itself. If you try to tell the teacher/examiner that you have enjoyed the subject, you will come across as dishonest.

ESSAYS ARE NOT PRIMARILY DESIGNED TO TEST YOUR KNOWLEDGE THEY ARE DESIGNED TO TEST WHETHER YOU CAN ANSWER THE QUESTION ASKED

All the points made above refer to essays in general. But in each of the subjects you study, the examiners will be seeking for what are good essays in their subject. Special considerations will apply in each subject. The History examiner will be looking for sound analysis of the basic facts, citation of primary sources where appropriate, etc. The Psychology examiner will be looking for a grounding in observational or experimental evidence, provided by citation of empirical research, etc.

The special requirements of the examiners for good grades in each subject are listed in the criteria for evaluation of essays, provided for the use of examiners and available to schools. You should be aware of the special requirements of the examiners in each of your subjects.

ENSURE THAT YOU ARE AWARE OF THE SPECIAL REQUIREMENTS FOR GOOD ESSAYS IN EACH OF YOUR CHOSEN SUBJECTS AND ToK

Interpreting the Question

Read the question very carefully. make sure you understand it before you begin to plan your answer. In the Chapter on Studying in a Foreign Language there is a list of the key words used in examinations in English, together with what they require. If in doubt, refer to it.

The Essay Plan

There are two forms of useful essay plan:
● the detailed plan made for an essay done at home;
● the simple plan for an essay during an examination. (You will not have time for more.)

In general, your plan should be simple:
● introduction,
● main body,
● conclusion.

There is an old saying, that you should:
● write about what you are going to write,
● write it,
● write about what you have written.

Correctly understood, this is a wise policy to follow if you cannot think of anything more appropriate to the particular question you are answering, for the chief concern of the teacher or examiner will not be how much you know, but whether you know how to answer the particular question asked. You can tell him this in the introduction by repeating the question in your own words and by giving a brief plan. In the conclusion, you can show exactly how you have answered the question. This need involve no unnecessary repetition.

Introduction

An introduction may include:

- a reformulation of the question in different words, (but make sure it *is* the same question);
- a brief outline of the essay plan;
- a quotation which illustrates the nature of the problem;
- definitions of the key terms;
- challenging the terms of the question. Do not be afraid. When done convincingly, it earns respect. e.g. If the question says: "Was Hitler an ideological fanatic or a self-interested opportunist?" you can argue that these two categories are not mutually exclusive, and that he could have been both, perhaps at different times.

Main Body

In the main body of the essay:

- Develop a line of argument as fully as you can (with one main topic or idea per paragraph).
- Do not repeat yourself in the main body of the essay
- Flesh out the skeleton of your argument. Cite evidence and arguments to explain and justify the points you have made. It is not enough merely to assert them.
- Confirm your ideas wherever possible by referring to published materials, properly cited (see below).
- Clarify what you say with examples, graphs or diagrams where appropriate.
- At all times keep in focus the precise question you have been asked to answer, and the main themes of your argument.
- Only write what is directly relevant to answering question.

Conclusion

Ideas for conclusions include:

- your conclusions about the arguments you have deployed (which side you come down on, and why);

- an account of exactly how you have answered the question set;
- a quotation which succinctly sums up your conclusion.

Constructing Arguments

Most essays should take the form of considering various ways to analyse an issue. Mere description or narration will almost certainly be insufficient for a high grade.

Many issues may be analysed in one of two ways. These are best answered by:

- stating the issue;
- presenting the arguments or evidence for one point of view;
- presenting the arguments or evidence for the other;
- weighing up the arguments or evidence and coming to a conclusion.

Make sure that when you are stating an opinion, you make it clear that you recognise it *is* opinion, and not fact.

Psychologically it is more satisfactory if the arguments (or evidence) for the point of view that you decide is the best one are presented last. Being the most recently read, they will tend to appear more convincing, and therefore leave the impression that your conclusion is soundly based.

Where an issue may be analysed in many ways, or when there are many competing explanations, the following plan is advisable:

- state the issue;
- present the arguments for the various viewpoints;
- weigh them against each other;
- come to a conclusion.

Each individual point may be developed by:

- stating it;
- explaining it;
- giving examples;
- justifying it by citing evidence.

Again, the best explanations should generally be placed last, before the conclusion.

Style

The style appropriate for essays in each of your subjects will vary somewhat, but some general advice can be given:

- Write as clearly as possible. Confusion of expression is usually an indication of, and a consequence of, confusion of thought. Try to think clearly exactly what it is that you want to say, and then say it as precisely as possible.
- Avoid rhetorical flourishes or "purple passages" which might be appropriate in a political speech or religious sermon, but which are out of place in an academic essay.
- Do not use note form in essays; i.e. sub-headings or numbered paragraphs, unless these are generally acceptable in the subject you are studying.
- Do not use "I." Write impersonally. e.g. Do not write: "I think that the foundations of Stalin's totalitarian state were laid by Lenin." Write: "It can be maintained that the foundations of Stalin's totalitarian state were laid by Lenin." Alternatively: "There is persuasive evidence that the foundations of Stalin's totalitarian state were laid by Lenin." The essay for Theory of Knowledge and some essays for Language B will be exceptions to this rule.
- Use guarded language. Avoid "it is certain that . . ." "it is obvious that . . " unless it really is. And it rarely is. Do not normally claim that you have "proved" something in an essay. Restrict use of the term "proof" to mathematics or philosophy (and in Philosophy, use it very carefully). Instead, use such phrases as "it is probable that . . ." "it is likely that . . ." "it is reasonable to suppose that . . ." For a very strong position say something like: "The weight of the evidence points over-whelmingly towards . . ."
- If you are working at home, read your essays aloud to yourself to be sure that the language is not awkward, and that it "flows" properly. If it does not, you will hear it.
- Scholarly writing demands complex sentence structure. Use colons, semicolons and commas to create richer, and more complex sentences.
- Use the technical language of your subject. This will:
    - help demonstrate your grasp of the subject to the teacher/ examiner;
    - help you express your ideas succinctly.
- Omit needless words! If a word or phrase can be dropped without a change in meaning, drop it. If a word adds irrelevant

information or no information, omit it. Adverbs such as "rather", "quite", "somewhat", "truly", "honestly", and "very" are usually irrelevant. Students get into the habit of using certain words, e.g. "actually," "however," quite unnecessarily. If a rephrasing will eliminate several words, use the shorter phrasing. Look out for such alternate phrasings.

- Don't attribute human qualities to non-human objects. While this is a useful, and effective technique in fiction writing, it is usually inappropriate in scholarly writing. The effect may be unintendedly amusing. The most common instance of this is attributing intentions or actions to the paper you are writing: "This paper demonstrates" and "This study will attempt to show."
- Keep a scholarly tone. Don't become too passionate, too carried away with your topic. Don't use sarcasm, mockery, satire, snide commentary, quips, asides, or exclamation points. Give both sides of any issue. Remain objective and analytical. Don't get on a soap-box. Scholarly writing is just not the place for preaching or zealotry.
- Never use slang, jargon, clichés, or any other colloquial expressions appropriate only in the spoken language. Use only formal language. Avoid contractions like "don't" except in quotations for direct speech.

Citations

Citation shows where the ideas or quotations you have used come from. This is so that the evidence you have cited in defence of your argument may be checked.

Reference to your sources may be made in the text. Where X is an author cited and Y the work cited, the following phrases are useful:

As X points out . . .
As X shows in his . . .
As X draws our attention to . . .
In his Y, X states . . .
X argues . . .
X suggests . . .
X makes the point that . . .
X argues . . .

Formal citation is made either by using footnotes or endnotes, or parentheses. The style conventionally used varies from subject area to subject area. Minimal information is given in citations; just enough to identify the book or article in the bibliography, together with the page, or pages, from which the ideas or quotations are taken.

In arts and humanities essays, cite in brackets using the author's surname and the page number of the work cited; e.g. (Petrides, 217). The citation may instead be made in exactly the same way, but inserted as a footnote at the foot of the page, or as an endnote on a separate sheet of paper at the end of the text. If this is done, superscript arabic numerals should be used, and the notes are numbered consecutively throughout the text. In social science and science essays cite in brackets using the author's surname, followed by a comma; the year of publication, followed by a colon, and the page(s) referred to; e.g. (Papadopoulos, 1984:17) This may be used in arts and humanities essays to avoid confusion if more than one work by the same author is cited. In the unlikely, but by no means impossible event that you are citing two works by the same author in the same paper, add an "a" after the year of the one that occurs in the bibliography first, and a "b" after the second: e.g. (Papadimitropoulos, 1997a: 212).

In addition to bibliographic citations, endnotes or footnotes may be used for additional information which may disrupt the flow of the text or the readers' concentration. Thus they may be used for:

- Additional relevant biographical information on an important figure;
- Definitions of key terms used;
- Opposing points of view;
- Minor qualifications of the main argument;
- Cross references to other parts of the text or to appendices;

Endnotes and footnotes should be reasonably short. Large amounts of information should be placed in appendices.

Who Are You Writing For?

It is important not to:

- State what is obvious to anyone over the age of four years, thereby insulting the intelligence of the teacher/examiner, and gaining no credit;
- Omit important material which you take for granted, but which you must demonstrate to the examiner that you know.

For this reason, you should write as though for someone who is:

- As intelligent as you are;

- Has a normal amount of common sense;
- Knows almost nothing about the precise you are writing about;
- Wishes to understand it, but has not had the privilege of attending your I.B. course.

Your own Opinions

Essays in the arts and social sciences usually require that the student take up a position on the matter under consideration. The student is asked for his own opinion. This is a great problem for some students who cannot see anything in between, one the one hand, merely parroting someone else's opinions, and on the other, expressing one's own unsupported and arbitrary preferences.

Marks are not awarded simply for having an opinion. Anybody can have an opinion on anything at all. It does not follow that such an opinion is worth anything. To be of value, and to be awarded credit, the student must present and support a reasoned position:

- The student's opinion must be clearly and elegantly expressed;
- There must be some justification for the student's preference, and this must be based upon the weighing of the arguments or evidence.
- Alternative positions, together with the arguments and evidence for them, must also be adequately discussed;

It is, of course, quite permissible for you, after carefully weighing up the arguments and evidence for various possible positions, to conclude that the arguments are evenly balanced, or the that the evidence is simply insufficient to draw any definite conclusion.

**THE SINGLE MOST IMPORTANT SKILL
WHICH WILL DETERMINE YOUR SUCCESS
AT UNIVERSITY OR COLLEGE
IS YOUR ESSAY WRITING ABILITY.
IMPROVING YOUR WRITING ABILITY
WILL PAY FOR ITSELF A THOUSAND TIMES OVER.**

Originality and Plagiarism

Your essay must be your own work. That is the justification for you getting the credit for it. For this reason, plagiarism is considered a serious offence in schools and colleges. It may be punished by zero marks, a reprimand, or even more serious disciplinary sanctions, depending upon the seriousness of the offence. It is therefore important to know what it is.

Plagiarism is passing off someone else's written work as one's own. This might be by:

- getting someone else to write the essay;
- copying someone else's work, either published or not, without acknowledgement.

Students sometimes think that this means that their writing must be original. This is not a simple issue. There are many different senses of "original." Very little ever written is original in the strongest sense: that no one has ever thought of it or written about it before. All popularising books and journals, all school textbooks, including this one, and all encyclopaedias, are based upon original research previously written in monographs and academic articles. Ideas are continuously recycled.

It is precisely by being able to demonstrate that you can express cogently these ideas already in circulation and part of the scholastic/academic tradition, that you demonstrate to the examiner that you understand them. Therefore expressing facts and theories which have been written about before is NOT plagiarism.

Plagiarism consists in:

- **Allowing someone else to tell you what to write.**

  Your teachers or others may in general *advise* you how to approach the task of writing an essay, but they may not tell you what to write, for then it becomes *their* essay and not *yours*.

- **Using someone else's exact words to express ideas, without enclosing them in quotation marks and acknowledging dependence.** When making a quotation from another person's work, you should acknowledge the source of the material by giving the author, the name of the book or article, and the page numbers.

  This rule needs to be applied with some common sense. There are not many different ways to say some things. Just because a textbook says "Mars is the fourth planet from the sun," it does not follow that if you choose to make this statement in your research paper, you must either put it in quotation marks or find some other way of saying it, such as "Mars is between the third and the fifth planet from the sun." But if you read some striking and engaging way of saying something, you should give the author credit for it by acknowledging your source, and putting it in quotation marks.

You should not use too many quotations in an essay, simply because the teacher/examiner wants *your* answer to the question, not a collection of quotations from other people's answers. Don't drop in strings of quotations unless they are evidence for your position or unless they are evidence from a passage you are subjecting to detailed criticism.

Some students include endless quotations from outside sources, and themselves provide enough original text only to tie together the quotations. Sometimes even that is not done well. This seems to be particularly tempting in Theory of Knowledge essays. You have to provide some evidence that you actually have actually thought about and understood the points made in your sources. You should summarise and paraphrase your sources wherever possible. This demonstrates your understanding of the issues.

For the same reason, you should not deliberately "borrow" entire paragraphs. Your quotations should be brief.

- **Failing to indicate the origins of an idea which is not common knowledge and not in general circulation.** A paraphrase of another person's ideas should also be shown by an acknowledgement. If the idea can be found in a score of textbooks, or could be elicited from a significant section of the population if asked the appropriate question, then it needs no citation.

Ideas are not private property, and should not be treated as such. Once they have been publicised, they have become part of the ongoing process of building up a store of human knowledge, to be acquired by each generation of students in their turn. But what is not common knowledge needs to be identified.

This rule also needs to be applied with common sense. What is common knowledge among physics students many not be common knowledge among students (and teachers) who have never been physics students. This issue arises in its most difficult form in connection with the Theory of Knowledge essay, where students, teachers and examiners alike may be dealing with issues outside their areas of expertise.

The best policy is to be overcautious and cite sources whenever you are in doubt as to whether it is necessary or not.

The Reasons for the Conventions of Quotation and Citation

It may help you to navigate through the difficulties here if you understand the two main reasons for demanding appropriate use of quotation marks, citations and bibliographies in students' essays.

- In academic work we seek to place our knowledge on a firm foundation. One way in which we do this is by the system of conventions of using quotation marks, citations and bibliographies. By these means, ideas and evidence can be systematically traced to their sources, and those sources examined and evaluated. in this way, in the sciences, the original observations and experiments can be identified, while in history the original primary sources can be located. This discipline needs to be acquired, and this is an important part of your education.

- Schools need to assess students' performance in order to assess the degree to which they have understood what they have been taught, while colleges and universities need to use grades and examinations in order to select students for admission to competitive institutions and courses. For this reason, it is necessary for them to judge work which is genuinely your own work. Plagiarism undermines this, in that the student who plagiarizes seeks to obtain credit to which he/she is not entitled, in competition with fellow students by submitting someone else's work as their own.

For this reason, plagiarism presents a particular problem in relation to all course work which counts towards the I.B. Diploma which is not assessed by formal examinations. Thus the greatest care is taken by the IBO to ensure that some students do not obtain unfair advantage over their peers by plagiarism. For example, examiners have access to software which will perform searches on the Internet, enabling them to detect if a student has copied and pasted material online. Examiners are also usually well-acquainted with the literature of their subject, and can recognise unacceptable "borrowing". In addition, the style of students' plagiarised work often gives them away.

There are many "grey areas" in deciding what counts as plagiarism and what does not. Since the consequences for a student who plagiarizes are draconian, it simply is not worth taking any risks. If there is any doubt in your mind, cover yourself by putting in quotation marks or by making citations.

BE OVER-CAUTIONS IN MAKING
QUOTATIONS AND CITATIONS
SO AS TO AVOID
THE SUGGESTION OF PLAGIARISM

Essay Checklist

When you have finished the essay, you should ask yourself:

● Have I answered the question asked (the question, the whole question and nothing but the question), as opposed to "dumping" my notes on the subject onto the paper?

● Have I structured the essay with an introduction, a clear line of development, and a conclusion?

● Do my first sentences convey the impression of someone who knows exactly what he is doing, and someone who is going to get straight down to doing it in an efficient and well-informed manner.

● Does my essay take the form of an argument, or is it merely an uncritical narrative of supposed events or description of supposed facts?

● Do I provide detailed evidence to back up my argument at each point it is needed?

● If the question is controversial, have I referred to scholarly opinions on the matter?

● Have I used the technical terminology of the subject wherever appropriate?

● Have I demonstrated that I have a viewpoint of my own on the issue?

● Is my spelling, punctuation, grammar and syntax correct?

● Have I written with elegance and panache?

● Is the essay of the length specified by the teacher or examiner?

● Have I provided the requirements of the I.B. criteria for essays of the highest grade in its subject?

Taking Tests

In order to ensure gaining the maximum marks do not try to answer the questions in the order set. You will end up wasting time trying to think of the answers to questions which you cannot answer, and you will find yourself at the end of the test having failed to reach questions which you could easily have answered. Thus you lost marks you could easily have gained. Instead:

- First answer those questions you can answer straight away;
- Then answer those which require some thought.
- Leave to the end those which you think you cannot answer. Then, as a last resort, make an intelligent guess.

In this way you will make the best use of the time available, and not risk running out of time before you have answered all the questions you could answer.

Short Answer Questions

It is important that you are aware what is being tested by the short answer questions. This may be:

- Knowledge of background information
- Your comprehension of a passage
- Your ability to analyse a passage
- Your evaluation or critical appreciation of a passage
- A mini-essay

There are some important points to follow in answering short-answer questions:

- It is especially important to consider the number of marks awarded for each of the questions, which may be very different.
- If a question carries one mark, it will usually require one point of information in response, although this may be complex. If you know the answer, you must write it down briefly and clearly. This

will usually require a single sentence. Any more than that will usually be irrelevant "padding" and will earn no extra marks. If you are in a hurry because you have a problem with time, then a single word may be sufficient to gain the mark. If you write a full page, the examiner will not extract the correct answer out of what you have written. he will conclude that you do not know how to answer the question.

- If you don't know the exact answer, but you do know something related to it, write down what you do know. You may get partial credit for it. If you don't know the correct answer, make an informed and reasoned guess.
- If questions are in several parts, you must pay attention to each, and answer each part.
- Be concise. Generally, short answer questions are testing specific knowledge, and are marked for content rather than style.

Objective Tests

Objective tests are tests in which all the answers are clearly either one thing or another. They involves no complications or subtleties of judgement, so that, theoretically, a computer could mark the test.

True or false Questions:
- Remember that for a statement to be true, it must be entirely true. Absolute terms like "never", "always", "only", "necessary", "must", etc. are rarely true; while relative terms, such as "like", "often", "seldom", "perhaps", "generally", etc., are often true because they are used to claim less.
- Take especial care with double negatives, e.g. "There is no time when this is not true."

Matching Pairs:
- Match the easiest things first, i.e. the ones you know, and cross them off.
- Using the process of elimination, do the best you can with whichever words are left in each column.

Multiple-Choice Questions:
- First try covering up the answers offered and anticipating the correct answer.

- If this does not solve the problem, read all the answers given. Do this even if the first or second one seems right. They may both be correct, with the last choice as "all of the above."

- If you are not certain of the correct answer, then "reverse into" it. First cross out the answers you know are not right, then choose the better of the remaining answers. Usually two answers out of four are obviously wrong. Another will be the "trick" answer, deliberately laid to mislead you.

- If you cannot recognise the answer among the alternatives not eliminated, always choose what appears to be the "best" answer. This is often the one that uses a technical word or phrase specific to the course.

- Never say: "The answer couldn't be C for the third time in a row." It might be.

- Finally, unless there is a penalty for incorrect answers, make a guess. Do not leave any questions unanswered. A few minutes before the end of the examination you should guess the answers to all the questions you were unable to answer.

Data Response Questions

These are questions based upon a passage, table of statistics, document, etc.

- Read the questions first, so that you will be alerted as to what to look for when reading the data.

- If the data is in the form of a written passage, read it over once, quickly, looking for the main idea, for what the passage is about in general. Ignore the details. Ask "What is the author trying to say?" Try to ignore unfamiliar words.

- Try to work out the meanings of unfamiliar words from the context.

- Re-read more slowly and carefully for structure, looking for the main divisions of the passage. Draw a line across the page after the introduction. What are the main points the author makes in leading up to his thesis, or in justifying it? You will find in a longer essay that you may have to deal with groups of paragraphs, all having to do with the same aspects of the main subject. Draw lines between the main groups and give the groups labels. Some paragraphs may be purely illustrative; while others may just contain comments digressions by the author. Some will be transitional paragraphs, taking us from one point to another.

- Identify the topic sentence of each important paragraph and mark it. Sometimes the topic sentence is at the beginning and sometimes at the end. Sometimes it is only implied.
- You now have the outline of the author's argument and should be able to follow his reasoning
- Finally you may have to consider other questions: why did the author write this, and for whom? What audience did he have in mind? What assumptions did he make, i.e., what did he take for granted his audience already knew, or already believed, or both?

After the Test

Ask yourself:

- Did I read the questions properly?
- Did I manage the time available properly?
- Was my question-answering strategy properly put into effect?

When the test has been marked, scrutinise your corrected test and ask yourself:

- Where can I improve?
- Did I really understand the questions?
- Did I explain the answer fully?
- Which questions did I find difficult?
- Were they all on the same topic?

Do not be depressed if you make a mess of a test. Use it as a learning experience. Learn by your mistakes and resolve to do better next time.

Working in the Laboratory

Laboratory work is intended to help you acquire skill and confidence in:

- learning how to handle and use scientific equipment and instruments;
- learning experimental techniques and procedures;
- developing the skills of:
    - making observations;
    - measuring with an appropriate degree of accuracy;
    - recording your observations and measurements in appropriate forms;
  - interpreting your observations;
  - writing up reports of experiments;
  - making inferences from your observations;
  - developing the ability rationally to defend your conclusions;
- developing your ability to identify those questions which are appropriately investigated by experiment;
- so laying the foundations for later academic and professional expertise in the experimental sciences.

Personal Protection

The science laboratory is potentially a dangerous environment. Equipment, materials processes may injure seriously. Therefore your first concern should be the safety of yourself and your fellow students.

- Wear the safety glasses and any other protection provided.
- You should not wear contact lenses, particularly soft lenses. They can hold chemicals in the eye, increasing the possibility of damage if chemicals are accidentally splashed into the eye.
- Shoes, and not open-toed sandals, should be worn.
- Do not wear clothing which would be expensive to replace.

- Long hair and loosely hanging clothes should be secured.
- Eating and drinking, in fact, tasting anything, in the laboratory is potentially dangerous.
- Be aware of the meaning of the warning symbols used in your school.
- Make sure that anything you touch is not hot.
- When the Bunsen burner is not in use, switch it off or adjust it to show a luminous flame.
- Notify the teacher immediately in case of an accident, no matter how small it seems.

General Laboratory Rules

Careless and inappropriate behaviour may cause accidents.
- Always conduct yourself in a mature and responsible manner. Horseplay in the laboratory is dangerous.
- When entering the laboratory, do not touch any equipment, chemicals, or other materials in the laboratory area until you are instructed to do so.
- The tables should be as uncluttered as possible.
- Do not set equipment too close to the edge of the table.
- The aisles should be kept clear to prevent tripping, so that other people can pass unhampered. Place book bags etc. under the lab tables or leave them outside.
- Carefully follow the directions of the teacher. If you do not hear or understand them: then ask. Make sure that you understand instructions before doing anything at all.
- Know where all the safety equipment is located.
- Never perform any practical work alone. If an accident happens, you will need to rely upon assistance.
- Never perform unauthorized experiments; the results may be catastrophic. Students have been killed in this way.
- If you are asked to design an experiment, never carry it out without first having it approved by your teacher.

In the Physics Laboratory
- Only use equipment for the purposes for which they were intended.
- Any equipment not in use should be turned off.
- Do not take apart any apparatus or piece of equipment

- Do not activate any circuit or apparatus by yourself. Wait for the teacher to inspect it.
- Do not short the electrical leads on any equipment.
- Hands must be dry when touching electrical equipment.
- Never look directly into the beam of a laser.
- Never play with the containers of radio-active materials.
- Ensure that your table top is covered with absorbent paper when dealing with radio-active substances.
- Do not work with radioactive materials if there is a break in the skin below the wrist.
- Wash hands and arms thoroughly after handling radio-active materials.

In the Chemistry Laboratory
- Check labels on bottles before using their contents.
- Replace stoppers immediately, and keep bottles away from the edge of the bench and from your elbows.
- If anything spills or breaks, inform the teacher immediately.
- Assume all chemicals to be dangerous unless you know other-wise. Handle them only under the direction of the teacher.
- Keep flammable and combustible materials away from flames.
- Take special care when handling highly flammable liquids.
- Be especially careful with concentrated acids. Never add water to them. Always add the acid slowly to the water.
- When heating something in a test tube, always slant it. The mouth of the test tube should point away from you and from others.
- When smelling a substance is required, do not hold it directly under your nose. Gently waft the odour towards your nose with your hand.
- When shaking a test tube, close the end with a bung or cork, never with your thumb or forefinger.
- Never fill a test tube which is to be heated more than one fifth full.
- Always use a pipette filter.
- When handling solids, use a spatula or forceps.
- Do not force glass tubing into a stopper. Use glycerine or water to lubricate the glass first.
- Always wash your hands after laboratory work.
- If you get any chemical on your skin or in your eyes, wash them

thoroughly and inform the teacher as soon as possible.
- Never remove chemicals from the laboratory.

In the Biology Laboratory
- Notify your teacher before you begin of any health problems you have which may have undermined your immune system
- Avoid contact with preservatives.
- Rinse specimens completely before dissection.
- Never dissect a specimen while holding it.
- Handle scalpels and razor blades with great care. Always cut away from your body and away from others.
- Properly dispose of dissected materials.
- It is very important to wash your hands after each dissection.
- Never remove specimens or specimen parts from the classroom.

Good practice
In addition to preserving your and your fellow students' safety, you should develop the habit of following good practice in the laboratory.
- If you are working in groups, don't let the others do everything
- Take only as much material as you need for your experiment.
- Wash up as you go along. and keep your work area clean.
- Replace equipment and containers as you found them

Writing the Report
The following information should be included, although not necessarily in this order:
- Aim
- Materials and equipment used.
- A drawing of the experimental set-up.
- The precautions taken.
- The procedure followed, and your observations of what happened.
- The results. Record accurately what actually happened, and not what you think that the teacher expects you to say happened.
- The calculations.
- Evaluation.
- Bibliography.

Your teacher may specify a particular variation of this list.

Studying in a Foreign Language

If you are taking a course in a language which is not your mother tongue, attending lessons, researching and writing essays and taking examinations in that language, you must also learn to think it. You must not constantly translate into and out of your mother tongue. This simply will not work.

> **LEARN TO THINK**
> **IN THE LANGUAGE OF YOUR I.B. COURSE**

Researching in a Foreign language

Since you are reading this book, we can assume that you will be taking the I.B. Diploma in English.

Researching in English

The following symbols may be found in English books, particularly in the footnotes and bibliographies:

anon	anonymous
c.	about (for an approximate date)
CF	compare
ch.	chapter
circa	about (for an approximate date)
ed.	editor
et al	and others (for books with multiple authors)
et seq	and what follows
f	and the following page

ff	and the following pages
ibid.	the work cited previously
idem.	the same page in the work cited previously
infra.	below
loc. cit.	the same page in the work cited previously
op. cit.	the work cited previously
p.	page
passim	in passing in several places
pp.	pages
(*sic*)	deliberate error
supra	above
tr. trans.	translation
vide infra	see below
vide supra	see above
vol(s).	volume(s)

Writing in the Language of your IB Course

Either write in your mother tongue or in the language of your I.B. course, but never mix the two. Do not allow one to influence the other. If you do, the result will sound barbarous both to speakers of your own mother tongue and to speakers of the language in which you are doing your I.B. course. For this reason, never write a paper required in the language of your IB language in your mother tongue first and then translate it. The result will be a barbarous mixture of the two languages.

It is best to write everything to do with your I.B. courses in the language of your I.B. course. This includes your own notes. In this way, you will come to think about what you are writing in the language of your IB course, which will aid you enormously when you have to think in that language in the examination room.

> **MAKE YOUR NOTES
> IN THE LANGUAGE OF YOUR IB COURSE**

You should not write essays in your mother tongue and they translate them into the language of your IB course. If you do:

- You will never learn to think in the language of your I.B. course
- The result will not read well.

If you have a computer, never use a translation software program. The result will inevitably be incoherent.

**NEVER WRITE ESSAYS IN YOUR MOTHER TONGUE
AND THEN TRANSLATE THEM
INTO THE LANGUAGE OF YOUR IB COURSE**

Writing in English

- There are differences between accepted styles in different languages. Scholarly writing in English aims first and last at clarity. Avoid the temptation to seek long and impressive words, when there are shorter words which will do the job equally well. Avoid "purple passages."

- If you are in a British school, use British spelling consistently. If you are in an Australian, Canadian or American course, use Australian, Canadian or American English for your spelling consistently. Never mix them.

- In English a paragraph is used for a single unit of thought; therefore a single point should be made in a single paragraph. (Of course it may be a matter for you to decide, in any particular context, what counts as a single thought). For this reason, do not be afraid of short paragraphs, and of a mixture of short and longer paragraphs. There is no reason at all why paragraphs should all be of similar length. If a particular paragraph is very long, it may be split up at some logical point, but different points should never be gathered together arbitrarily to make short several paragraphs into one longer one.

- Do not use contractions such as isn't, doesn't, etc., except in quotations.

- Always capitalise proper adjectives wherever they appear in a sentence, e.g. Greek, British, Albanian.

- Learn to use the apostrophe correctly. Apostrophes are never required merely to form a plural; only to indicate possession (This is Julian's book) or to replace missing letters removed in contraction (can't, doesn't, he's). Learn how an apostrophe is used to indicate possession with nouns ending in s and learn where the apostrophe is placed to indicate possession with plural nouns.

● Distinguish its from it's. These are very commonly confused. Take the time to learn the distinction so well that you never confuse them again. "It's" (with apostrophe) is only a contraction for "it is"; if you can replace the "it's" with the words "it is", then use the apostrophe. If you want to indicate possession with the pronoun it, as in "The college cares about its students," use no apostrophe. This contradicts the general rule for using "'s" to show possession, but is necessary to avoid confusion with the contraction of "it is".

● Distinguish "your" from "you're". "Your" is always possessive: "This is your book"; or "I'm your friend". "You're" is always the contraction for "you are": "You're going to fail the examination if you don't work harder."

● Distinguish "their" from "they're". "Their" is possessive: "This is their house"; "I'm not their servant". "They're" is always the contraction for they are: "They're so poor"; "they're going to lose all their money".

● There is no such construction as "could of" in the English language. What you want is "could have". Never write "could of", etc.

● English has many near-synonyms – words which mean almost the same thing as other words, but not quite. To take advantage of this, learn to use a thesaurus. This is a book which lists words of similar meaning. Whereas in a dictionary you start with a word and discover its meaning, in a thesaurus you start with a meaning and find a word for it. You look up in the index the word which is closest to your idea, then in the section on that word you find words of similar meaning to it. The most famous thesaurus is Roget's Thesaurus. Known universally by this name, and originally written in 1852, it is continually revised and updated to take account of changes in the language. Some programmes, such as Microsoft *Word*, now include a thesaurus.

Taking Examinations in English

If you are not sure what a question means, and you have a choice, it is probably wiser to choose another question, even if you know that topic rather less well. It will be better to get a lower mark answering a question you know you are answering correctly, than to risk getting a much lower mark for failing to answer the question set. Pay particular attention to the key words which are used in examination papers in English.

Key Words in Examinations in English

Account for	Explain why X is as it is.
Analyse	Describe the various elements of X and how they relate to each other and to the whole of which they are parts.
Comment upon X.	Describe and evaluate various points of view on X.
Compare X and Y.	Describe the major similarities and differences between X and Y.
Consider X.	Describe and evaluate various points of view about X.
Contrast X and Y.	Describe the differences between X and Y.
Define X.	Explain the meaning of X.
Demonstrate that X. . .	Provide a proof that X. . .
Describe X.	Give a detailed account of X.
Discuss X.	Describe and evaluate various points of view on X.
Enumerate X	Make a list of . . .
Estimate	Make an approximate calculation of the value of . . .
Evaluate X	Give a judgement, supported by argument or evidence on the value of X.
Examine X.	Describe the various elements of X, how they relate to each other and to the X itself.
Explain X	Give an account of why X is as it is;

Outline X.	Give the main points in an account of X, omitting details.
Relate X and Y.	Show and explain the connections between X and Y by comparing and contrasting them.
Review	Examine and evaluate . . .
Select	Choose . . .
Specify	State, list . . .
State.	Express clearly and concisely.
Summarise X.	Give the main points in an account of X, omitting details.
Trace.	Follow a line of development.

Working with Computers

Used properly, computers can be very useful tools for any student. Wherever possible, you should be able to use a computer, modem and printer. They are useful to:

- Make and store notes;
- Access information stored on compact disks;
- Research information on the Internet;
- Edit and present essays;

Computers allow you to:

- Edit successive drafts easily, deleting, adding and moving blocks of text. This is its most important function.
- Perform calculations;
- Display information graphically;
- Check spellings
- Count up the number of words
- Print out a paper in a presentable form.

Since computers are going to be so important to all of us in the future, the time spent on learning how to use one, although a considerable investment at the time, will certainly not be wasted in the long run. But don't waste time playing games when you should be working.

Backing Up

Give your files appropriate names. so that you can recognise what they contain easily. If you do not, it would be easy to lose files if you cannot remember what name you gave to them.

It is easy to lose work if your computer crashes or the power supply fails. For this reason, save your work every five minutes or so.

Important work should be backed up by being saved off the working computer, on a disk, CD rom or memory stick. Even then you may not be entirely safe. Many back-up resources fail. Very important work should be backed up on two media independent of the original computer and each other, and also in hard copy. (the printed version) You would not want your complete extended essay to be lost just before it was due to be handed in.

**DON'T TAKE RISKS
BACK UP REGULARLY**

Using the Computer and Your Health

Working on a computer for a long period of time can cause physical discomfort and health problems.

- Repeated or forceful bending of the wrist can cause painful inflammation of the nerves and tendons. This is due to prolonged use of the mouse and keyboard.
- You can get eyestrain.

To avoid problems, take the following precautions:

- Adjust your chair to find the most comfortable position for your work. Your forearms should be nearly horizontal. Your eyes should be the same height as the top of the monitor.
- Try to keep your wrists straight when using the keyboard. Keep a soft touch on the keys.
- Support your forearm on the desk.
- Don't grip the mouse too tightly. It isn't going anywhere. Rest your fingers lightly on the buttons and do not press them hard.
- Avoid glare, or bright reflections on screen. Neither you nor the screen should be facing windows or bright lights. Nor should the screen reflect a bright light behind you.
- Make sure that the screen surface is clean.
- Make sure that there is adequate space under your desk to move your legs about freely.
- Do not sit in the same position for long periods. Move your legs about frequently.
- Take frequent small breaks.

Hints for Approaching Particular Subjects

Much of the advice given by teachers of the various subjects is the same from subject to subject.

In all your subjects you should:

- attend lessons regularly;
- review your lessons and your notes regularly;
- acquire and employ in your thinking and writing the technical vocabulary of the subject. This will:
  - demonstrate your grasp of the main concepts
  - make it easier to write essays and answer examination questions succinctly.
- hand in assignments carefully done and on time;
- engage in background reading to immerse yourself in the subject.

The following are hints for specific subjects:

Language A

Appreciation of a Text

Students sometimes misunderstand what is required in an "appreciation" of a text. This requires three stages:

- An initial appraisal
- A detailed analysis
- The final evaluation

Initial Appraisal:

- Consider the literal meaning of the passage. This requires that you read the text carefully in order to ensure that you have understood what the author said, and not what you *think* he said.
- What is the passage about?

- Consider the *tone* of the passage, how the writer feels about his subject matter and about what he is trying to do with his text. Ask such questions as:
  - Is the style formal or informal?
  - Is the author serious or flippant, solemn or light-hearted?
  - Is he approving or condemnatory?
  - Is he seeking to:
    - communicate information;
    - arouse emotions;
    - influence opinions;

He may have more than a single intention at the same time.

- To what *genre* does the passage belong?

Detailed Analysis:

This is an attempt to evaluate the degree of success with which the writer has realised his intentions by an analysis of the techniques the author has used. Among the techniques which should be considered are:

- Imagery. This may be for description, or it may function symbolically, to suggest meanings or evoke an emotional response.
- Diction, the associations the choice of words has for us;
- Rhythm. Prose has rhythm as well as poetry;
- Rhyme.

Final Evaluation:

This should assess:

- the extent to which author's style successfullky contributes to the realisation of his intention.
- the total impression the passage makes on the reader.

Writing Essays for Class Assignments and Examinations

Pay close attention to the requirements of the question:

- Questions requiring an account of scenes should not merely narrate the scene, they should show how those scenes contribute towards the development of the plot, and how they throw light upon the main characters.
- Character study questions do not require a simple account of that character's role in the plot. They require:
  - an analysis of role of that character in the development of the plot,

- the development of the character in the course of the working out of the plot.

Character traits should be presented in the order required by your general argument, and not in the order in which they appear in the text.

All the points you make should be supported by evidence from the text. If the question requires "quotation", then the exact words of the text must be supplied. If the question specifies "close reference" then it requires the substance of the text in your own words

Style in Literature Essays

- Underline (or print in italics) any titles you refer to. This is particularly important if the title has the same name as one of the characters. The examiner needs to know whether you are referring to the play *Macbeth* or the character Macbeth.
- Prose quotations should be set in the texts, while longer quotations should be set out separately from the main text, indented from the margin and without quotation marks. Poetry quotations of two lines or less should be inserted in the text, the lines separated by "/". Longer quotations should be set out as in the poem, indented from the margin and without quotation marks.
- References from plays should be set out as follows: Act V, Scene iv, lines 16-20 as (V.iv.16-20). Simple line references should be set out using the abbreviations "l" (line) and "ll" (lines), e.g. "l.6"; "ll.7-15".

Language B

Since the passages you work on, together with the essays you write, require acquaintance with the culture associated with the particular language you are studying for Language B, you should familiarise yourself with current newspapers and magazines from that culture and in that language.

Philosophy

Thinking philosophically does not come naturally. It is therefoire important to learn, as quickly as possible, to think in a rigorous, sustained and systematic way, and to get out of slack and shallow everyday ways of thinking. You must learn to focus rigorously upon the logical and conceptual aspects of an issue, and argument. Your essays must demonstrate rigorous, sustained, systematic thinking, securely based upon sound argument.

History

Essays

History, as studied for the IB diploma, is not simply a matter of learning what happened in the past, but it is about interpretations and explanations of what happened in the past. For this reason, your essays should never be mere narrative accounts, or even chiefly narrative accounts, of the past. Nor should they be biographies. They should be, from beginning to end, arguments about interpretations or explanations of the past. Narrative and biography should only come in as evidence in argument for or against particular interpretations and explanations.

Source Criticism

The criticism of historical sources is needed:

- On Paper I
- In the internally assessed study;
- For the extended essay;
- In general historical reading.

You should always refer to the origin and purpose of the sources you are assessing, and note both their value to historians and the limitations of their value.

Always make comparisons in your thinking between similar types of development in different parts of the world, e.g. between the causes of different wars, and between the nature of different single-party states.

Let your studies in History inform your understanding of the world today, and relate what you learn about international politics to the events and developments you learn about in the news.

Psychology

You should always be aware of the scientific method, as it is applied in psychology, in your own investigation.

Your essays should always be firmly based upon evidence, in the form of empirical studies, which should be cited according to accepted conventions.

Economics and Business Studies

You *must* pay especial attention to your basic mathematics skills, and ensure that they are up to the demands of these subjects.

You need to become aware of the environment in which businesses and the economy operate. This involves reading international and national newspapers and news magazines.

Mathematics

You have already read about progressive subjects. Mathematics is the progressive subject *par excellence*, in that each Mathematics class tends to build on the material learned in previous ones. Therefore you *must* attend class, keep up with the teacher, and do all the homework set. The problems help you learn the formulas and techniques you need to know, as well as improving your problem-solving skills. Falling a single day behind puts you at a disadvantage. Falling a week behind puts you in deep trouble. For this reason it is important that if you fail to understand something, you must recognise and admit what you have not understood, and put it right as soon as possible. If you do not, you will probably fail to understand the new topics you will do next, which may presuppose knowledge of the steps you have missed or failed to understand.

Problem Solving

Students frequently face difficulties with Mathematics problems because they have not adequately understood the theory on which the solutions to the problems will have to be based. Make sure that you understand the theory before you begin to try to solve the problems.

The higher the mathematics class you attend, the more types of problems you will encounter. In earlier classes just one step was sometimes required to find a solution. Increasingly, you will tackle problems which require several steps to solve them. Break these complex problems down into smaller steps.

A four step process is usually recommended for approaching mathematics problems:

- Identify exactly which quantity the problem is asking you to find or solve for; (make sure you read the whole problem).
- Identify which skills and techniques you have learned which can be applied to solve the problem.
- Apply them.
- Check that the answer you found seems reasonable.

Sometimes the problems don't appear very realistic, but that is usually because the corresponding real applied problems are too hard or complicated to solve at your current level. But at least you get an idea of how the mathematics you are learning can help solve real-world problems.

Applied problems should first be converted into mathematics.

- If possible, start by drawing a diagram. Label it with all the quantities mentioned in the problem.
- If a quantity in the problem is not a fixed number, name it by a variable.
- Identify the goal of the problem.
- Complete the conversion of the problem into mathematics, i.e., find equations which describe relationships among the variables, and describe the goal of the problem mathematically.
- Solve the mathematics problem you have generated, using whatever skills and techniques required, using the four-step process above.
- Convert the answer back into words, so that you have now solved the original applied problem.
- Make a rough estimate. This is a useful strategy for solving calculations, problems and checking your answers. Round off all numbers and mentally estimate the answer. This will tell you whether or not your answer is reasonable.

Studying for a Mathematics Test

- Review your notes on theory.
- Ask yourself what kind of problems you have learned how to solve, what techniques of solution you have learned, and how to tell which techniques go with which problems.
- Make flowcharts to understand and fix in your memory procedures for solving particular types of problem.
- Try to explain out aloud, in your own words, how each solution strategy is used (e.g. how to solve a quadratic equation). If you get confused during a test, you can mentally return to your verbal instructions. Check your verbal explanations with a friend (it's more fun than talking to yourself).
- Put yourself in a test-like situation: work problems from review sections at the end of chapters, and work old test papers. It is important to keep working problems the whole time you are studying.
- Check that you can still do the homework problems (actually work some of them again).
- Use the worked examples in the text and notes by covering up the solutions and working the problems yourself. Then check your work against the solutions given.

Test-Taking Strategy:
- In a multiple-step problem outline the steps before actually working the problem.
- Show all your working out. Make it as easy as possible for the teacher or examiner to see how much you know. Try to write a well-reasoned solution. If your answer is incorrect, the teacher or examiner will assign partial credit based on the work you show.
- Never waste time erasing. Just draw a line through the work you want ignored and move on. Not only does erasing waste precious time, but you may discover later that you erased something useful (and/or maybe worth partial credit if you cannot complete the problem). If you have erased it you will have to work it all out again.
- Be accurate. Check your operational signs (+,-,x, etc.) and numbers to avoid errors. Keep your place value columns lined up. Write all signs and numbers clearly.
- Any time you seem to beexpected to do an unusual amount of arithmetic in the time available, check whether it is really necessary or whether there is a better way of approaching the problem.
- Don't give up on a problem which requires several steps to complete just because you can't do the first part. Attempt the other part(s). If the actual solution depends on the first part, at least explain how you would do it.
- If you finish early, check every problem (that means rework everything from scratch).

Technology
Calculators
You should get acquainted with youtr calculator as quickly as possible. Read the booklet and learn how to perform the basic operations. Do not be afraid of it. Play with it, so as to become familiar with it.

However, do not become dependent upon it.
- Do not trust your calculator to provide correct answers.
  - Don't use the calculator hastily or carelessly. If you have large or ill-co-ordinated fingers, or your calculator is small, it is easy to press the wrong buttons.
  - Make sure that the memory is cleared between calculations.
  - Make rough estimates of your answers in your head or on paper to ensure that the answer your calculator gives is realistic.

- Get to know which operations it is best to do by calculator and which by mental and written operations.

Computer Programmes

Ensure that as soon as possible you are familiar with Microsoft *Excel*.

The Sciences

Experiments

Experimental investigations test a student's ability to:

- understand and follow instructions;
- construct a suitable hypothesis;
- plan and design an experiment;
- use scientific apparatus;
- make accurate observations;
- make accurate measurements;
- record observations accurately;
- present results in a suitable form;
- interpret the results correctly;
- make sound logical deductions on the basis of the results;
- Critically discuss the methods used and results obtained.

Writing a Scientific Report

A scientific report is generally divided into the following sections:

- Abstract,
- Introduction,
- Method,
- Results,
- Discussion,
- References.

It should be made clear by your use of your use of capital letters and underlining, (and on computer by your choice of font sizes) which are your main headings and which are your sub-headings.

Abstract: This should state in as specific terms as possible what experiment you carried out, what its results were, and what interpretation you placed on them. It is a summary of the report in a few words.

Introduction: The introduction should say briefly what you were trying to find out and why. It should relate your own work to existing knowledge. It may also contain a justification for the design of your experiments. It should lead up to a statement of your experimental hypothesis.

Method: Describe the subjects, apparatus, procedure and experimental design including the methods of analyzing the results. The procedure must be described in such detail that someone reading it would be able to reproduce exactly what you have done. Do not, however, include irrelevant detail. (What is relevant, and what is not, depends on exactly what it is you are doing.)

Results: Present the raw data, although a full presentation may be included in an appendix. Present the main findings at the beginning of the section and go into detail later. If there is an independent variable which entered into your analyses but was not significant (sex or order of presentation are typical examples) dispose of it early in this section. Present statistics in the conventionally accepted ways. Tables and graphs are usually the best way of presenting the data in a comprehensible form. Draw attention to those parts of your data that you feel are most important. The outcome of any statistical test should be included in this section.

Discussion: Assess the importance of your results and present your main conclusion. Relate your findings to your objectives set out in the introduction and to published research. Interpret your results in the light of existing theories. Draw attention to any weaknesses in your results or in the design of the experiment. You may also suggest what further experiments should be undertaken in the light of your experience.

References: All papers and books referred to should appear in the list of references and all references must be given in the same conventional form.

Appendices: These should be reserved for material which is not essential for understanding the report, but which provides further information. Examples of questionnaires used, for example, are best relegated to an appendix.

Music

Students should expose themselves to the maximum acquaintance with many different types of music, both in a practical way, in playing instruments, and in appreciation.

Theatre Arts

In Theatre Arts the student's portfolio matters a lot! The portfolio is produced by editing a journal, which should be kept throughout the course, although some new writing may be included to make connections between original entries and emphasise their significance. Obviously this journal needs to be BIG!

Both the journal and portfolio should focus on:

● Performance skills, as acquired and developed through the course

- Theatre Productions the candidate is involved in,
- Critical responses to external productions.

The portfolio should be a reflective and critical record of the candidate's own development through the course. Original journal entries should not be like 'class notes' in other subjects but should elaborate your experience of learning, especially in relation to those sorts of practical work which may be difficult to put into words.

Keeping a journal regularly (writing entries at least once a week) throughout the course is vital. Think of it as both a record of your learning and a learning tool to help you learn. Every couple of months go back over it and write about how things have changed for you since your earlier entries, if they have (and they should have!)

Visual Arts

You should be prepared to attend and interpret various opportunities for visual stimuli, such as art exhibitions, theatre, film, etc. In particular, you should take care to visit any art exhibitions which are available to you. If exhibitions are not accessible in your place of residence, you should try to substitute for this by using the resources of the Internet.

Always take your workbook and a small camera around with you in order to record your ideas and impressions throughout the day.

Computer Studies

You should spend about two hours a week programming at home.

Theory of Knowledge

Although Theory of Knowledge is not one of your six chosen subjects, its importance should not be underestimated. In many ways, the course in Theory of Knowledge lies at the very heart of the I.B. experience. That is why it is compulsory. A good performance in Theory of Knowledge is the mark of a well-educated student, one who is capable of benefitting from a university education in a demanding, intellectually competitive environment.

Making the ToK Presentation

(See the chapter "Making a Presentation.")

Writing the ToK Essay

Preparing the essay
- Note all the basic concepts which will need to be employed, and logical points which will need to be made, in order to provide an appropriate answer to the question. These may not always be apparent in the wording of the question.

Writing the Essay
- Any absolutely crucial concepts should normally be clarified, perhaps defined, very early on in your essay.
- Clarify the other key concepts as they become relevant.
- Be inventive when choosing illustrative examples. Choose examples from different subjects and different cultures wherever this is appropriate.
- It is entirely appropriate to use the word "I" in a ToK essay, when referring to your own experience as a knower.

Final Work
- Check your facts.
- Support all facts which do not count as not "general knowledge" with footnotes and a bibliography. Be aware that this is a "grey area" and so be prudent. If you are in any doubt, make citations and include a properly set out bibliography at the end.
- Read through your essay with the ToK criteria in mind. Adjust what you have written to earn maximum marks.

Creativity, Activity, Support (CAS)

You should look upon your CAS activity not only as something which you have to do, but also as something which is:
- useful;
- enjoyable to you.

For this reason, you should find an activity which:
- interests you, e.g. with people or animals;
- looks good on your *curriculum vitae*;
- is reasonably accessible from your home.

If you choose your activities wisely, you may learn a lot which you could never learn in school, including from those you may be trying to help.

Making Connections

On the IB course you should always be aware of the connections which can be made between different parts of the syllabus within a particular subject, and between your various subjects. e.g. You will use some of your Mathematics in physics, economics and psychology. Connect your economics and history to throw more light on both of them.

You do not study your various subjects simply to amass marks in the IB examination. You should use your school learning to help you better understand the world in which you live. e.g. Make connections between what you learn in history and economics with current events and the international news.

Making Presentations

Near the end of your Theory of Knowledge course, you will have to make a presentation to the class, either alone or with others. You will probably feel anxious about it. However, be confident. If you have done your preparation, then you will probably know more about the subject of your presentation than most of your audience will.

Planning

Planning, preparation and practice are crucial. Planning a presentation involves:

- Deciding what you want to talk to the audience about (clear objectives)
- The points will you want to put over - the main headings and components points and their sequence
- Working out how those points can be put over best.

If you decide to make your presentation with others, make sure that they are people you can cooperate with.

- Use a similar structure as for planning an essay:
  - introduction,
  - main body,
  - conclusion

Apply the ancient rule:
  - First you tell them what you're going to tell them;
  - Then you tell them;
  - Then you tell them what you have told them.

- If you are doing it in a small group, make sure in your planning, that everyone will take an adequate part in it so that each person taking part can be given a mark for what they have done. No single person should dominate the presentation if a group is doing it together.

- Do not plan to read from a script, although you should have some notes in front of you. Reading from a script is specifically forbidden by the I.B. Regulations. So if you go ahead and do it anyway, you are not going to get much for it.

> **WRITING AN ESSAY**
> **AND READING IT OUT**
> **DOES NOT COUNT AS A PRESENTATION**

- Do not stay up late planning it the night before. It will not be well planned, and you will not be in a good state to deliver it.
- Be aware of the criteria by which the presentation will be assessed. Take this into account during your planning by "building into" your the content of your presentation the requirements for the highest marks.

> MAKE SURE THAT YOUR PRESENTATION
> **BEGINS** WITH A PROBLEM OF **KNOWLEDGE**
> **IS CENTRED UPON** A PROBLEM OF **KNOWLEDGE**
> AND **ENDS WITH** A CONCLUSION ABOUT
> A PROBLEM OF **KNOWLEDGE**

- Don't fill your presentation with too much detail. Distinguish between which points it is essential to make, and which points can also be made if there is time.
- Take special care over the closing section. it will create the over-whelming impression you will leave people with.
- Practice your delivery beforehand.

Aids to Presentation

In order to make your presentation interesting to your audience, you can incorporate a range of audio-visual aids.
- Photocopied handed out

- Illustrations on paper displayed before the class
- Illustrations on acetate for an overhead projector
- use video/DVD
- Computer generated presentations using Power Point, etc.
- Debate
- Taking Questions
- Drama
- Display of art or science exhibits.
- Questionnaires

Make sure:

- You really know how to use any equipment and any computer software that you are going to employ, how it might go wrong, and what you would do to put it right.
- If you exhibit any small objects or printed material of any type in front of the whole class, make sure that it is large enough for the people at the back to see it.
- Give out any handouts before you start, or have someone give them out for you unobtrusively. Stopping your presentation to hand things around breaks peoples' concentration.

Remember that it is the content of the presentation, relative to the criteria, which counts, not the variety and magnificence of the audio-visual aids employed.

On the Day

- Arrive before most people are in the room.
- Wait until everyone is quiet before beginning.
- Don't hurry. Start after a deep breath and continue at an even pace, slower than your normal speech.
- If you find yourself taking lots of short, shallow breaths, just pause for a minute and breathe in deeply.
- Pause briefly at the end of each section, to give your audience time to absorb what you have said.

IF YOU ARE NERVOUS, REMEMBER:
**IT'S ONLY YOUR FAMILIAR ToK TEACHER
AND YOUR USUAL CLASSMATES**

- Speak loudly enough for everyone to hear comfortably. Speak to the back of the room.
- Change the cadences of your voice. Don't speak in a monotonous drawl.
- Be enthusiastic. Enthusiasm and interest are infectious.

IF YOU CANNOT DISPLAY ANY ENTHUSIASM
FOR **YOUR** PRESENTATION
WHY SHOULD ANYONE ELSE?

- Involve the audience -- look at them. Don't talk at your desk.
- Adjust your material to suit the time. Keep an eye on the teacher to see if this is a problem. Don't gabble if you find yourself seriously over-running. Summarise instead.
- Make sure that the main points do not get lost in the detail.
- Don't distract people by nervous mannerisms, such as pacing backwards and forwards, tapping your foot on the ground, etc.

If there is a question and answer or discussion stage:

- Change your position, move towards your audience but maintain eye contact with everyone.
- Ask for comments and seek clarification if you do not understand someone's question.
- Bring your audience into the discussion
- Don't be defensive.
- Control the discussion to keep questions broadly on the subject.
- If you take questions, and you don't know the answer to a particular question, then say so. It won't be a disaster, and you will earn everyone's admiration for your honesty. Anyway, no one can be expected to know everything.
- A standard way to end is to smile at your audience and say, "Thank you."

After the Presentation

Fill in the self-evaluation report as soon as possible afterwards, while everything is still fresh in your mind. Don't forget to hand it in.

The Extended Essay

The I.B. Diploma requires the submission of a research essay called the extended essay. The individual subject requirements may also specify a similar piece of research which will deserve considerable attention and effort.

Unlike an examination, when you do not know in advance exactly what the questions will be like, the extended essay may be on a subject chosen by you, and can be prepared for and worked on at length. For this reason, there is rarely a good excuse for a student to submit a poor extended essay.

The examiner will be looking for evidence of:

- the ability to organise and plan a piece of research;
- the commitment necessary to carry it out;
- an understanding of the central issues involved, and that the student has disentangled the central issues from peripheral ones.
- an ability to communicate these in a clear and readable form.
- an acquaintance with the formal and conventional requirements of written research.

Unfortunately students too often put off starting their extended essay and internally assessed research papers, considering them too formidable to approach until a late stage. Because these are substantial tasks, you should resist the temptation to put them off, because they will require a considerable investment of time and effort. If you leave them until the last moment, your papers will be rushed and poor, and this will affect your score.

The Stages in Preparing the Extended Essay

Writing the extended essay involves several stages:

- Familiarise yourself with the I.B. Extended Essay General Guidelines

- Choose the subject in which you will do your extended essay (e.g. History, Physics)
- Familiarise yourself with the Subject Guidelines.
- Choose a topic;
- Locate sources of useful material;
- Do preliminary reading to survey the topic;
- Choose a research question
- Make detailed notes;
- Make an outline;
- Write the first draft;
- Show it to your supervisor for his comments;
- Revise and edit the text;
- Illustrate it (if necessary);
- Write the abstract;
- Proof-read the final version;
- Show it to your supervisor again;
- Produce the final version for submission.

The teacher who supervises your extended essay is allowed to:
- give you advice on the topic;
- indicate possible sources of research material;
- advise you on the general approach;
- indicate and help you with skills you will need;
- indicate problems in your draft and suggest solutions.

He may NOT edit your draft.

YOU WILL GET THE CREDIT FOR YOUR ESSAY
THEREFORE YOU MUST WRITE IT
YOUR SUPERVISOR CAN ADVISE
HE/SHE CANNOT DO IT (OR EDIT IT) FOR YOU

If you leave it to the last minute to show a draft to your supervisor, you cannot expect him to give you useful comments on it; there will not be time to do anything about it.

Making Initial Choices

Choosing a Subject

You may choose a particular subject because:

- You wish to develop as strong a background in the subject as possible before applying to, or going to, university to study it;
- You are interested in the subject;
- You would have liked to have taken the subject for the examination, but for some reason were not able to.

Choosing a Topic

This should be:
- Within the specifications allowed by your supervisor;
- as specific as possible;
- interesting to you. (You are going to have to do the work.)
- clearly lie within a single specific subject area. It cannot be an interdisciplinary topic, one that spans the subject boundaries.
- require the handling of expensive equipment or dangerous substances.

Choosing a Research Question

The Essay should be written as an answer to some particular question. This is known as the research question. You should never choose:
- Issues for which you do not know that there is sufficient material accessible to you to upon which to base your research. Some preliminary survey of available material may be advisable before the research question is chosen.
- Issues in which you are not really interested. You will have to invest considerable time and energy on the project.
- Research questions which require only a narrative, a biography or description in response, since such an essay will usually be awarded low marks.
- Speculative questions, since these are unanswerable. e.g. "What would have happened if King George I of Greece had not been assassinated in 1913?"
- Compound or multiple questions. e.g. "Are U.S. high schools nationalist, racist, sexist and homophobic?"
- Questions which carry questionable implications: "Why are U.S. high schools homophobic?"
- Interdisciplinary questions, which do not clearly fall within a single subject area.
- Questions which embody the requirement to make value

judgements, e.g. "Was the dropping of the atomic bombs upon Japan by the USA justified?"

- Questions which you have answered, or intend to answer, and submit for assessment for another requirement of one of your courses. This does not include class assignments set by your teacher as part of your normal schoolwork.

If you choose a question which might come up on an examination paper, you would be well set to provide an answer in the highest mark band, since you will know more about it than most students. But this is provided only that you are capable of employing your knowledge in such a condensed way that you do not spend too much time answering this question, and lose time to answer the others properly.

The Thesis Statement

In response to the research question you may wish to adopt a particular standpoint towards the subject matter you are writing about. This may be expressed in a single statement, known as the thesis statement. The thesis of the essay will need to be supported by evidence. The presentation of the evidence to support the thesis statement constitutes the main argument of the essay.

Take care not to make the about your standpoint too soon, i.e. before you have surveyed the literature on the subject. It my lead you to ignore evidence contrary to the standpoint you have chosen, and so will limit your essay. A good plan is to leave it to the end. It should be your conclusion.

Locating the Information

In order to acquire the information necessary to write your essay, it will be necessary to research the subject. you have chosen The first problem is to locate suitable source material. The teacher may advise you on books or other material which may be used, and where to obtain them. If not, you will be expected to find suitable material for yourself.

Some books may be purchased. Certainly, you should get into the habit of owning books, many of which will prove useful and give you pleasure in future years. In non-English speaking countries, the purchase of books delivered in the post and paid for by credit card on the Internet may solve some of your problems. You should order early, so as to leave time for the books to get to you, especially if your local postal service is unreliable.

Wherever possible, for most resources, you should make yourself acquainted with the available libraries. If you have access to the Internet may also be able to find relevant and helpful data online.

Depending upon the subject you have chosen, there may be other sources of information which you can draw upon, such as the data of your own investigations, the oral testimony of people to whom you have access, etc. Consult your supervisor about the suitability of these sources, together with any special precautions you need to take in using them.

You may find that there are not sufficiently adequate sources to enable you to write the essay you wish. You must then change your research question or topic as soon as possible. Never put this decision off.

Researching in Libraries

The first thing to do upon entering a library is to find out whether it will be of any use to you

● Are there any restrictions on who can use the library, e.g. by age;

● Whether it is a specialist or a general library, and has books on your topic.

You will need information on:

● Opening hours;

● Whether it is an open access library, where anyone can pick out and use books, or a closed-access library, where books have to be applied for and are brought to you to use;

● The system used by the library to classify books;

● The location of the library catalogues;

● How to use the catalogues to find the material you are seeking;

● The location of study areas, where notes can be made on the books;

● The location of reference books;

● The location of journals (current issues and bound volumes);

● Whether books may be borrowed, how many, and for how long;

● Whether there are photocopying facilities, and how much they cost to use;

● Whether books not in stock may be ordered, how long they will take to arrive.

The Library Catalogue

The library catalogue contains a complete list of all the books, periodicals and other sources of information (newspapers, micro-fiches, videocassettes, CD-ROMs, etc) available in the library. It may take the form of a large cabinet containing drawers full of small cards (called "catalogue cards"), a collection of loose-leaf binders, CD-ROMs or information stored on a computer hard drive, and accessed from computer terminals linked in a system.

The books in the library's collection will usually be listed in the catalogue by author, title and subject. You can use the library catalogue:

● to find the place on the shelves where all the books about your topic are to be found;

● to locate specific books.

Books are normally searched for by author's name. If you do not know the name of the author of the book you are seeking, only its title, you will look up its title card. Note that when books are looked up under title, the indefinite and definite articles are placed at the end; otherwise most books with English titles would be found under "The", "A" or "An". A typical catalogue card for the title of the same book might look like this:

By using the subject entries, you are able to find out the authors and titles of all the books in the collection on any given subject. This makes the subject entries particularly helpful for students seeking to learn what books the library has in stock on the particular subject they are researching. To access a book using the subject card you will need to understand the system of book classification used in the library.

You will need the information given on the cards:

● To locate the books on the shelves;

● To enter in your references and bibliography if you are writing a formal essay.

Systems of Book Classification

In order that books on any subject can be located quickly, they will be classified according to some system. It is important that you find out what this is when you first arrive, so that you will be able to find what you want on the shelves. The two most common systems of classification used in libraries are the Dewey Decimal system and the American Library of Congress system, although some specialist libraries may have developed their own methods.

The Dewey Decimal System

Books are first classified into one of ten groups by being given a three figure number from 000 to 999.

000-099 General, Reference and Books on Books
100-199   Philosophy and Psychology
200-299   Religion
300-399   Social Sciences
400-499   Language and Languages
500-599   Mathematics and the Pure Sciences
600-699   The Applied Sciences and the Useful Arts
700-799   The Fine Arts and Recreation
800-899   Literature
900-999   Geography, Biography and History

Within each hundred the classes are divided into ten sub-divisions, e.g.

500-509 General Science
510-519 Mathematics
520-529 Astronomy
530-539 Physics
540-549 Chemistry

Each subdivision is divided into ten further subdivisions.

590   Zoology
591   Animal Habits and Behaviour
592   Invertebrates
593   Sponges, Corals and Jellyfish
594   Molluscs
595   Other Invertebrates (animals withoutbackbones)
596   Vertebrates (animals with backbones)

Subdivisions of these classes are represented by figures after a decimal point, e.g. 527.942.

In larger collections, the decimal number may be followed by the first three letters of the author's surname, e.g. 942.36WAN.

The Library of Congress System

Increasingly, libraries all over the world are adopting the system of the American Library of Congress. Listed below are the letters and titles of the main classes of the Library of Congress Classification.

A – General Works
B – Philosophy, Psychology, Religion
C -- Sciences Auxiliary to History
D -- History: General and Old World
E -- History: America
F -- History: America
G – Geography, Anthropology, Recreation
H -- Social Sciences
J -- Political Science
K -- Law
L -- Education
M – Music, Musicology
N – Fine Arts
P – Language, Languages, Literature
Q – Science, Mathematics
R -- Medicine
S -- Agriculture
T – Technology
U – Military Science
V – Naval Science
Z – Library Science

Within each area there are further subdivisions which are represented by numbers, e.g. in Class Q – SCIENCE:

Q 1-385	Science (General)
300-385	Cybernetics. Information theory
QA 1-939	Mathematics
9-10.3	Mathematical logic
75.5-76.95	Computer science. Electronic data processing

276-280	Mathematical statistics
297-299.4	Numerical analysis
440-699	Geometry
611-614.97	Topology

QB 1-991	Astronomy
140-237	Practical and spherical astronomy
275-343	
Geodesy	
349-421	Theoretical astronomy and celestial mechanics Including tides
460-466	Astrophysics
468-480	Non-optical methods of astronomy
495-991	Descriptive astronomy Including stellar spectroscopy, cosmogony

QC 1-999	Physics
81-114	Weights and measures
120-168.85	Descriptive and experimental mechanics
170-197	Atomic physics. Constitution and properties of
matter,	
220-246	Acoustics. Sound
251-338.5	Heat
350-467	Optics. Light Including spectroscopy
474-496.9	Radiation physics (General)
501-766	Electricity and magnetism
770-798	Nuclear and particle physics. Atomic energy. Radioactivity
801-809	Geophysics. Cosmic physics
811-849	Geomagnetism
851-999	Meteorology. Climatology

Subdivisions of these classes are represented by figures after a decimal point. In larger collections numbers following the decimal point may be followed by the first three letters of the author's surname, e.g. BX265.21CHE.

The Reference Collection

A part of the library will be set aside for reference materials. These will usually include:

- encyclopaedias,
- dictionaries,
- directories,
- atlases,
- statistical compilations,
- periodical indexes and abstracts.

Reference books usually cannot be taken out of a library.

Some collections consist mainly of documents, such as government records. Collections of documents are called archives, and the person in charge of them is called an archivist. Because original unpublished documents are not only valuable historical and sociological records but are also unique, great care is taken to preserve them undamaged. For this reason, as a school student, you will normally be barred from consulting archives. If you are admitted to an archive, perhaps with the special permission of the archivist and a letter of recommendation from your headmaster. you may be required:

- to wear gloves,
- to use only pencil while in contact with the documents.

This is to prevent damage to the documents.

Appropriate Behaviour in Libraries

Libraries are places set aside for reading and study. Anyone who disturbs other people by rowdy or selfish behaviour is likely to be ejected, and barred from readmission. Anyone who even looks as though he or she is likely to cause such problems may be refused admission. For that reason it is advisable, when you intend to visit a library:

- not to dress in an unusual or eccentric manner;
- not to go along with friends, who may wish to talk to you;
- not to take into the library anything to eat or drink;
- always to behave in a quiet, businesslike and courteous manner.

Reading for Research

Unless you already know something about the topic you are writing about, it is generally a good idea to start by reading something elementary, which covers the whole field, so as to get a general overview of the topic. In general, encyclopaedias are not acceptable in the bibliographies of research papers, but encyclopaedia entries may provide good initial starting points, since they will provide a general picture of the topic which will allow you to get your bearings. Basic school text-books may also provide a good overview. These sources will help you understand the broad area of your research and tell you in general terms what is known about your topic. However, they should not be cited as sources of information in footnotes, not listed in the bibliography.

In searching for more detailed material, it will be necessary to search through large numbers of books and articles. There is not the time to read through all this material in the normal fashion. It is necessary only to scan it.

Use the contents and indices of books to find material more quickly. The contents page of books written in English is usually found at the front of the book, after the title page, although the practice in some non-English-speaking countries is to put it at the end. The contents page lists chapter headings. Analytical tables of contents are particularly useful, since they break down the contents of each chapter, section by section.

Evaluating Source Material

Initial Evaluation

Evaluating a source can begin even before you have it in your hand. You can initially appraise a source by first examining the details given about it in a bibliography in another book, or on its library catalogue card. These will provide you with its author, title, and publication information. These components can help you determine the usefulness of this source for your paper.

Author:

- What are the author's credentials: educational background, past writings, experience in the field? Is the book or article written on a topic within the author's area of expertise?

- Has your teacher mentioned this author? Have you seen his name cited in other sources or bibliographies? Respected authors are cited frequently by other scholars. For this reason, always give specizal attention to those authors whose names appear in many different sources.

- Is the author associated with an institution or organisation? Is it a university or college? If it is not, is it a political or religious organisation. Does it have links with big business. If so, what are its basic values or goals? What is its *angle*?

Date of Publication:
- When was the source published? This date is often located on the face of the title page below the name of the publisher. If it is not there, look for the copyright date on the reverse of the title page. On Web pages, the date of the last revision is usually at the bottom of the home page, sometimes every page.
- Is the source current or out-of-date for your topic? Topic areas of continuing and rapid development, such as the sciences, demand more current information. On the other hand, topics in the humanities often require material that was written many years ago.

Edition or Revision:
- Is this a first edition of this publication or not? Further editions indicate that a source has been revised and updated to reflect changes in knowledge, include omissions, and harmonise with its intended reader's needs.
- Many printings or editions may indicate that the work has become a standard source in the area and is reliable.

Publisher:
- If the source is published by a university press, it is likely to be scholarly.
- Although the fact that the publisher is reputable does not necessarily guarantee quality, it does show that the publisher may have high regard for the source being published.

Title of Journal:
- Is this a scholarly or a popular journal? This distinction is important because it indicates different levels of complexity in conveying ideas.

Analysis of Source Content

Having made an initial appraisal, you should now examine the body of the source.
- Read the Preface to determine the author's intentions for the book.
- Scan the Table of Contents and the Index to get a broad overview of the material it covers.
- Note whether bibliographies are included.
- Read the chapters that specifically address your topic.

Consider the following:

Intended Audience:
- What type of audience is the author addressing? Is the publication aimed at a specialised or a general audience?
- Is this source too elementary, too technical, too advanced, or just right for your needs?

Objectivity:
- Is the information covered fact, opinion, or propaganda? It is not always easy to separate fact from opinion. Facts can usually be verified; opinions, though they may be based on factual information, evolve from the interpretation of facts. Skilled writers can make you think their interpretations are facts.
- Does the information appear to be valid and well-researched, or is it questionable and unsupported by evidence? Assumptions should be reasonable. Note any errors or omissions.
- Is the author's point of view objective and impartial? Is the language free of emotion-rousing words and bias?

Coverage:
- Does the work update other sources, substantiate other materials you have read, or add new information?
- Does it extensively or only marginally cover your topic?
- Does it present a review of various viewpoints, or does it view things from a single perspective?
- Is the material primary or secondary in nature? Primary sources are the raw material of the research process. Secondary sources are based on primary sources. Choose both primary and secondary sources when you have the opportunity.

Writing Style:
- Do you find the text easy to read, readable with difficulty, or impossible to read?
- Are the main points clearly presented?

Reviews
Find critical reviews of books in periodicals.
- Is the review positive?
- Is the book under review considered a valuable contribution to the field?

- Does the reviewer mention other books that might be better? If so, locate these sources for more information on your topic.
- Do the various reviewers agree on the value or attributes of the book or has it aroused   controversy among the critics?

Making Research Notes

Good research notes are essential for writing a good research essay.

Skim through your sources, locating the useful material, then make good notes on it, including quotations and information for footnotes. Do it thoroughly. You do not want to have to go back to these sources again.

Ideally, you should make your notes on separate cards or sheets of paper for each author -- identifying your sources carefully.

There are two forms of research notes:
- Bibliographical Notes, which identify your sources;
- Subject Notes, which:
- summarise points made on the topic you are researching;
- include verbatim quotations you may wish to use;
- identify other possible sources of information you may wish to follow up.

Bibliographical Notes:

If your note comes from a book, it is necessary to record:
- The catalogue number of the book in the library (so that you can find it again)
- The author's name
- The title
- The publisher's name
- The place of publication
- The edition
- The date of publication

These should be obtained from the catalogue or from the book itself.

The catalogue number of the book in the library is essential so that you will be able to find the book again if you need to go back to it to check something, if you discover that you need more information out of it, or if you need to read it again to criticise it. All the other material except the page numbers is necessary for the bibliography. The page numbers are necessary to make citations if you use the notes in writing the essay.

The catalogue number of a library book is usually written on the spine.

The details required for the bibliography are to be found on the title page and the imprint page.

The title page of a book is the page on which the title of the book and the author's name appear in largest print. The publisher's name and the place of publication will usually be found at the foot of that page.

It is absolutely essential, when making notes for an essay or research paper, to make an exact record of the source of each note that you make at the time you make it. You will need these for your references. If you do not, you will find yourself having to revisit the libraries you have used to comb through the books there, trying to find the source you made your notes from in order to provide the references for them in the essay. You may also yourself need to go back to the source of the note for further information or clarification.

Since they will have only little time when they can visit a library, because in some countries the libraries tend to close when the schools do, school students will probably wish to make the amount of time they spend in a library as short as possible. This can be done by making photocopies, wherever possible, of passages which will definitely be useful. Most libraries charge for this service. If you do this, it is most important that you write full bibliographical details on all the photocopies you make, otherwise you will have to return for them later. There is nothing worse than having to return to a library, seeking out from the stacks all the books you have made notes on, and trying to find the pages where the notes came from. You will always be left with a residue that somehow you just cannot relocate. Save yourself the agony. Do it right the first time.

On the reverse of the title page, further information may be found. This is known as the imprint page, and contains the symbol ©, which means "copyright." On this page will usually be found a history of the publication of the book. The will include the date of first publication.

A book which is quickly sold out in the shops will be reprinted, perhaps many times. Each reprint is sometimes called an impression. The dates of the successive reprints or impressions are recorded on the imprint page. Sometimes the publisher decides that the book needs a new look. This may be to update or correct the information contained in it, or to alter its appearance in some way. If this happens, a new edition is said to have been published. The new form is called a second edition.

A popular book, in addition to being reprinted many times, may appear in successive editions. Since the text of a new edition may be different from that of the original, and since what appears on one page in the first edition may appear on another page in the second, it is necessary to refer to the specific edition which you have used in your references and bibliography. If no reference is made to an edition, it is assumed either that the first edition is referred to, or that there has only been one edition.

The impression page also bears the name of the printer and the place of printing. This information may be ignored. It is the name of the publisher and the date and place of publication which is important, not the details about the printer. Similarly, it is information about editions which is required, not information about reprints.

If the book is a collection of separately written articles in a book or journal, it is necessary to record:

- The catalogue number of the book in the library
- The name of author of the article
- The title of the article

**MAKE FULL BIBLIOGRAPHICAL NOTES
WHEN YOU ARE IN THE LIBRARY
SO THAT YOU DO NOT HAVE TO RETURN LATER**

- The name of the book
- The editor of the book (if there is one)
- The publisher's name
- The place of publication
- The edition
- The date of publication
- The page numbers of the article

All this information will probably be required later on.

For an article in a journal, it is necessary to record:

- The name of author of the article
- The title of the article
- The name of the journal
- The volume number
- The issue number

- The date of publication
- The page numbers of the article

Each year the journal receives a new volume number. The issue number refers to the issues which appear during the year. Thus Vol. III (2) will refer to the second issue during the third year of publication.

Subject Notes

You should observe all the precautions for making notes, detailed above. In addition:

- Make sure that you have understood the author, and that your notes do not distort his meaning.
- Do not merely collect only those things that will support your thesis, ignoring other facts or opinions. You will also need to consider other viewpoints.
- Get facts, not just opinions. Compare the facts with author's conclusion.
- It is absolutely essential, when making notes for a research paper, to make an exact record of the source of each note that you make at the time you make it. You will need these for your references. If you do not, you will find yourself having to revisit the libraries you have used to comb through the books there, trying to find the source you made your notes from in order to provide the references for them in the essay. You may also yourself need to go back to the source of the note for further information or clarification.

Since they will have only little time when they can visit a library, because the libraries tend to close when the schools do, school students will probably wish to make the amount of time they spend in a library as short as possible. This can be done by making photocopies, wherever possible, of passages which will definitely be useful. Most libraries charge for this service. If you do this, it is most important that you write full bibliographical details on all the photocopies you make, otherwise you will have to return for them later. There is nothing worse than having to return to a library, seeking out from the stacks all the books you have made notes on, and trying to find the pages where the notes came from. You will always be left with a residue you cannot relocate. Save yourself the trouble. Do it right the first time.

- Impose a time limit on your research. At some point you will have to stop collecting information and begin to write the first draft. Resist the temptation to go on searching for ever.

```
┌─────────────────────────────────────────┐
│        DO NOT LET YOUR RESEARCH          │
│           GET OUT OF CONTROL             │
│        STOP AT AN APPROPRIATE TIME       │
└─────────────────────────────────────────┘
```

Writing the Paper

The First Draft

Virtually no one is capable of writing out a research paper at one sitting. You will begin with a first draft. The notes have to be put together in the right order for writing out the essay – something which is only possible if they have been made on loose-leaf sheets or cards.

Do not bother, at this stage, with an introduction. Get down the body of your notes in the form of continuous prose. This is the basis from which you will gradually build your paper.

Your first thoughts might be quite sketchy. For a first draft this is perfectly acceptable. Then as you work on the draft you will need to flesh out the material used. You make a claim but to this you will need to add evidence, and ensure that you note the sources of all reference examples and a full explanation of what you mean. This is where your draft begins to grow. The important thing at this stage is to get something down.

If you use a personal computer, it is better to type the first draft straight onto the computer so that piecemeal revisions can be made on screen, rather than by rewriting the entire text.

```
┌─────────────────────────────────────────┐
│   DO NOT HAND IN A POOR, HASTILY WRITTEN,│
│               FIRST DRAFT                │
│       AND THEN EXPECT YOUR SUPERVISOR    │
│   TO TURN IT INTO A GRADE "A": ESSAY FOR YOU│
│       HE/SHE IS NOT ALLOWED TO DO THAT   │
└─────────────────────────────────────────┘
```

The Title

Choose this when you have written out the final version. Make it as precise as possible. Very short or enigmatic titles may only confuse and irritate the examiner. On the other hand, don't make it too long either. Look at examples of research titles appropriate to your level to get an idea.

The Introduction

Although the introduction comes first, there is no law which says that what is read first has to be written first. The introduction may be written last of all. It should explain to the reader why you did the study in the particular way that you did. The following is a suggested plan:

● General overview:
● why the topic is important and/or interesting
● A very brief outline the study. This will involve a formulation of the research question and thesis statement.
● the main theoretical and/or practical issues involved in answering the question;
● any aspects of the question excluded in the interests of narrowing down

The Argument

● Don't present opinion as fact.
● When you make an assertion, you should have an outside source to support it. You may not even want to assert seemingly obvious points; often these are less obvious and more controversial than you thought. It is best to refer to an outside source. You can then present outside viewpoints and perhaps synthesise a conclusion from them, or juxtapose them for contrast and express your own interpretation, or you could extrapolate, or do many other things to express your own take on the topic. But start with outside references. That way, you have someone else to point to when your reader asks, "How do you know that?"
● Don't rely on intuitive conclusions or impressionistic evidence to make a point.
● Don't use specific incidents as support for sweeping assertions. You may provide examples to support a point, but they should be representative of many other possible examples. Don't take an example and draw a conclusion from it. This is bad logic.

Editing

When you have finished your first draft you have taken perhaps the most satisfying step towards creating your research paper. But you will need to edit and perfect what you have created. This editorial work can be very, very time consuming. So don't relax at this point and then leave things to the last minute.

Revise your first draft several times. As you do this, constantly ask yourself:

- Does the report actually answer the research question?
- Is all the content relevant? Are there any sections where the relevance of what you have written is unclear?
- Is the order or sequence of the argument a good one?
- Are all the main points covered in sufficient depth?
- Is each main point adequately supported with argument, explanation and examples? Are any supposed facts or assumptions questionable? Do some positions lack support and require further evidence?
- Are there any inconsistencies; where what you have said in one part of your essay contradicts what you have said in another. (Do not forget that you are supposed to report all major viewpoints, and these may contradict each other. This is not a problem. It is when you contradict yourself that a problem arises.) Inconsistency is a major problem in large pieces of work, like the extended essay.
- Is there a clear distinction between ideas which are your own, and those which are taken from other people? Are all sources cited?
- Is it always clear what you mean to say? Is the language under control? Is your choice of words always appropriate?
- Are there any vague or unclear points which require some clarification?
- Is the grammar, syntax, punctuation and spelling correct?

Then put the problems right. It is necessary to do this several times, and a good idea to look for different things each time.

It is important to allow autosave to back up your work at regular intervals in case of a power failure. A careless movement of the foot or finger can result in the sudden cutting off of power or an unintended deletion, losing your latest revisions and perhaps an hour's work. Your work should also be saved on a diskette on completion of each revision session.

You should also number each copy so that you do not get confused and save an earlier revision over a later one.

**IF YOU ARE EDITING ON COMPUTER,
SAVE A COPY OF YOUR WORK
AFTER EACH REVISION
THEN PUT THE COPY IN A SAFE PLACE**

At this stage, do not worry about the length of your paper. Ideally, it should be too long, so that during the process of editing over-elaborate sections be made more concise. A paper written to its required length usually does not read as well as one originally written to a greater length and then condensed. The latter appears to be "packed" with material, and written by a student who could, if he wished, have written much more.

Only in the final stages of editing should you begin to worry about length. Then, if what you have is much too long, and even condensation does not reduce it to the required length, you can take advantage of the fact that the word limit which has been set does not usually include title page, acknowledgements, contents, footnotes, appendices, or bibliography, but refers only to the main body of the text. It is usually possible to:

- Place lists, tabulated material or very long quotations in appendices;
- Place less important subordinate arguments or supporting evidence in the footnotes.
- As always on the IB, write to the assessment criteria (general and subject specific). Look carefully at the descriptors which determine the characteristics necessary for an essay to be awarded the marks within in the highest mark band, and try to provide what is required.

AS ALWAYS ON THE IB DIPLMA COURSE WORK TO THE ASSESSMENT DESCRIPTORS

Style

This is much more formal than in the normal class essay.

- Do not use subheadings, or if you do, use them very sparingly. They are appropriate for notes, not essays.
- Use the technical language of your chosen subject.
- Underline (in manuscript or typescripts) or place in italics (on computer) all foreign words and titles in your text.
- Place all formulae and equations on their own lines, and identify each with a number in brackets on the right hand side for ease of reference in the text. e.g.

(4) $e = mc^2$

- Avoid abbreviations in the text, except AD, BC, e.g., etc. and i.e.., although in some subjects, further abbreviations are conventionally acceptable.

- Quotations should be:
- Short: The teacher and examiner want to read what you have written; they do not want to read what someone else has written.
- Useful: They must express a point or constitute evidence for a point. They should not be used merely as a show of erudition or to fill space. That will annoy the examiner.
- Telling: Direct quotation should be used because some position is expressed so pithily and so succinctly that you can use it to encapsulate a complex position in a few memorable words.

All quotations should be followed by a citation of the source.

Citations

Citations are particularly important in the extended essay., They:
- show where the ideas or quotations you have used come from. This is so that the evidence you have cited in defence of your thesis may be checked.
- show, if made correctly, that you have acquired this basic research skill.

In addition to bibliographic citations, endnotes or footnotes may be used for additional information which may disrupt the flow of the text or the readers' concentration. Thus they may be used for:
- Additional supplementary information which would break the flow of the text;
- Minor qualifications of the main argument;
- Definitions of key terms used;
- Opposing points of view;
- Cross references to other parts of the text or to appendices;

Endnotes and footnotes should be reasonably short. Large amounts of information should be placed in appendices.

Make citations using one of the accepted forms on pp.62-3.

Illustrations

Illustrations make a paper more informative, interesting and attractive. They should, however, only be used in serious work if they inform more conveniently or efficiently than text would.

All illustrations should be:
- placed either as close as possible to the first reference to them in the text; or if they would be so intrusive that they would break the thread of the argument, then they should be placed in an appendix at the back.

- labelled clearly; (Figure 1 or Table 1).

Such illustrations might include: photographs, scale line drawings: suitable for recording scientific observations, plans and maps. Particularly useful for displaying statistics are: text tables, arrays, histograms, barcharts, pie charts, cartograms, pyramids and graphs. Include graphs if, and only if, they will help the reader to understand. Graphs are not evidence in their own right; they are merely visual aids. Thus graphs should not be used to illustrate statistics if they are harder to understand than the statistics themselves.

- Choose an appropriate form of graphics
- Choose an appropriate scale
- Explain them with a legend or interpretation of shading or colours used. In the case of graphs, both axes should be clearly labelled.
- Don't clutter them.
- Use graph paper on which to construct your graphs, although you may trace the result onto clear paper so as to eliminate the grid lines on the graph paper.

Photocopies of photographs, maps, graphs, etc. may be used by individual students for their own research, provided that the source is acknowledged.

- Use clean, clear photocopies;
- Crop and mount them;
- Cut off the original labels, and assign labels which conform to your own numbering system.

Modern computer software has made the addition of presentable illustrations to essays comparatively easy, and increasingly, new developments are likely to make the process much easier still. But the student should beware losing valuable time, and of having his attention diverted away from his real task of producing a good piece of writing. The mechanics of producing fine illustrations using clip art, scanned photographs or other software created illustrations is found by many to be an absorbing activity, but is should be regarded as recreation rather than serious study.

Computers allow graphics to be introduced directly onto the page without being affixed in any way. Photographs and drawings may be downloaded from the Internet or, if already in the possession of the student, they may be scanned and converted into binary form. These may then be inserted into a text document, and subsequently printed out directly onto the page from the computer. Using such programmes as Microsoft *Excel*, data entered on spreadsheets may be converted into graphs: column graphs, line graphs and pie charts, etc.

Any illustration which is taken from a published work should be acknowledged in the same way that you would acknowledge the source of a quotation.

Before including illustrations, it is advisable to find out whether they will be appreciated. Generally, unless they are necessary to understand the text or themselves constitute evidence for the thesis of the essay, they will be regarded as undesirable. Illustrations designed only to make the presentation look pretty, or worse still, to disguise the poverty of the essay itself, will usually not succeed in influencing the final mark and may even be penalised.

> **USE ILLUSTRATIONS**
> **ONLY TO ILLUSTRATE SUBSTANTIAL POINTS**
> **IN YOUR ARGUMENT,**
> **NEVER FOR MERE DECORATION**

The Conclusion

This may be quite brief. It should follow from the arguments and evidence you have deployed in the body of the essay. Any questions which remain unanswered, or any further issues raised by your findings, should be indicated.

Bibliography

In the bibliography, all the information about books and articles used necessary to identifying them and locating them in libraries must be provided. For some subjects, all the books and articles consulted may be listed. In others, only those which have been cited in the text may be included. In this case, the list is often headed "References" or "Works Cited," rather than "Bibliography." You must, however, make sure that every book or journal article that you refer to in the paper appears in the bibliography.

The bibliography must be written out in accordance with the standard conventions. These conventions are established ways of doing things which have been found useful over the years. They vary a little, but not much. You must adhere to them because people will expect you to do so, and they will be upset if you do not, because it inconveniences them. Like all conventions, the conventions of bibliography may be broken. But if you break them you will suffer for it. Therefore, if you want the examiner to give you the maximum marks he can, you must follow them. In some examinations marks are awarded precisely for observing these conventions.

- Different types of source, e.g. books, interviews and Internet sources should be grouped separately.
- The works should be listed in alphabetical order of authors' surnames.
- When listing several books by the same author, you need not repeat the author's name each time. Instead, type the author's name in full for the first entry only. For subsequent entries, type three hyphens and a full stop, leave two spaces and then enter the title.

Word Count

Ensure that the word count for your essay is within the limit laid down in the regulations (4,000 words at the time of going to press). Only words in the text count. This excludes the abstract, bibliography, appendices and footnotes or endnotes.

If you find that you have too many words:

- Rewrite sections in a more brief and succinct way. Do not omit substantial points in the argument. Combine several related points made in several separate sentences into single complex sentences.
- Move subsidiary points into footnotes/endnotes.
- Transfer a single large amount of supporting material, such as verbal testimony from an oral source, into an appendix.

The Abstract

This is a short description of the essay. It is not part of the essay proper, and it should be inserted immediately after the title page. It should be brief, clear and not contain a single unnecessary word. It should include:

- The research question
- The thesis statement, and a description of how it is developed.
- A statement of the limits of the study.
- A description of any major problems encountered.
- A critical note of the various types of sources used.

It should be the last thing to be written, when you know exactly what the rest of the essay will contain in its final form.

Bibliographical Format

There are two sets of conventions with minor variants, the first is followed in the sciences and social sciences, and the second in the Arts. (All words set in italics here should be set in italics on computer, but underlined on manuscripts and typescripts.)

Sciences and Social Sciences

Books:
- Author's name (surname followed by first names or initials, as they appear in the book)
- Date of publication (in brackets)
- Title (in italics) A sub-title is added after a colon.
- Place of publication (city)
- Publisher's name (without such additions as "& Co. Ltd.")

Schneider, J. T. (1994). *Insane in America: a Study of the U.S. Mental Health Service.* New Jersey: Psycho Press.

Edited Books:

Some books are made up of chapters each written by different authors, which have been collected together into a single volume by an editor. These are introduced by the editor's name (followed by (Ed.): Schnelling, A. D. (Ed.) (1992). *Exploring the Mathematics of Four-Dimensional Space.* Manchester: University of Manchester Press.

Article in an Edited Book:
- Author of article
- Date of publication
- Title of article
- Title of book
- Editor of book
- Title (underlined or in italics)
- Place of publication
- Publisher's name

Masterson, J. (1991) "Learning to Cooperate: a study of sibling rivalry among young chimpanzees." In L. Werner (Ed.). *The Socialization of the Young.* New York: Zoom Press. 75-94.

Books in several volumes:
Schonnbrunnstein, G. (1974) *A Brief Military History of Modern Austria,* Zurich: Schickelgruber Press. Vol. xxxiv.

Books with several authors:
Beetleheim, R. G. and F. Schwarz. (1974) *The Romance of Cement Technology.* New Jersey: Simpson Books.

Books with more than three authors:
The first author only is given, followed by et al, meaning "and others": Schlesinger, James, et al. (1992) *Elementary Nuclear Fission.* New York: Proton Press.

Articles
Article in a Journal:
The basic pattern is:
- Author's name
- Date of publication (in brackets)
- Title of article (in quotation marks)
- Journal (in italics)
- Volume number (in italics)
- Issue number (in brackets). This is not necessary.
- Page numbers.

Schnellhausen, F. (1954) "Aggressive behaviour among garden snails in Provence," *Zoological Quarterly, 25*: 262-334.

Newspaper Articles:
Signed Newspaper Article:
Clough, Alisdair. (1995, Nov 19). "Exciting Developments in Sanitary Ceramics." *Potters' Gazette.* Stoke-on-Trent. 7.
Unsigned Newspaper Article:
"The Enigma of Cold Fusion." (1993 May 21). *Iowa Daily Review. 6.*

Encyclopaedias:
Signed Encyclopaedia Article:

Schnietzel, Wilbur. "Intelligence." *Encyclopaedia Americana.*
(1992) London: Mahler, Springster & Muller.
Unsigned Encyclopaedia Article:
"Protozoa." *Encyclopaedia of Science.* (1961) London: Fenton
Press.

Pamphlet, undated and without indication of publisher:
Dzhugashvili, I. V. (n.d.) *How to Cope with Recalcritant
Subordinates.* Moscow: (n.p.)

Humanities and Arts

Books:
● Author's name (surname followed by first names or
initials, as they appear in the book).
● Title (in italics). If there is a subtitle, place a colon
after the title and add the subtitle in italics.
● Publisher's name (in brackets)
● Place of publication (in brackets). If the book is
published simultaneously in many places, include only one.
● Date of publication (in brackets).
Wilson, C. *The Use of the Comma in the Nineteenth Century
Novel.* Oxford: Oxford University Press, (1988).

Edited Book:
● Editor's name
● Title
● Publisher's name
● Place of publication
● Edition
● Date of publication
Cavendish, T. (Ed.) *William Shakespeare to Arnold Bennett: the
Great Tradition of English Literature.* Stoke-on-Trent: Hanley
Press, (1985).

Article in an Edited Book:

- Author of article
- Title of article
- Title of book
- Editor's name
- Publisher's name
- Place of publication
- Edition
- Date of publication

Maybury, C. "Weeds in Shakespeare's *Richard II*." In Newton, R. *The Significance of Gardens in Shakespeare's Earlier Plays*. Birmingham: Stratford Press, (1954).

Article in a Journal:
- Author's name
- Title of article (in quotation marks)
- Journal (in italics)
- Volume number (in italics)
- Date of publication (in brackets)
- Pages

Wittlesbach, W. N. L., "Do Hallucinations Exist or Are They Hallucinations?" *Philosophers World, 54* (1993) 45-76.

Newspaper Articles:
Signed Newspaper Article:
Howard, Julian. "Saving the Lost Churches of Umbria." *Times.* (15 June 1998): 7.

Unsigned Newspaper Article:
"Uncovering the Lost Civilisations of Ancient Britain" *Staffordshire Guardian.* (29 August 1985): 9.

Encyclopaedias:
Signed Encyclopaedia Article:
"Marxism-Leninism." *Encyclopaedia of Political Science.* London, Engels Press. (1992)

Unsigned Encyclopaedia Article:
"Crusades," *Encyclopaedia of History*, London, (1991)

Poem in an Anthology:

Hartington, Elspeth. "Ode to a Dead Gorilla." *The Poetry of Bereavement: a Late Twentieth Century Anthology*, Eds. C. Spar and J. P. Newleigh. Cheltenham: Poesy Press, (1986). 66.

Unpublished Manuscript:

- Author's name (surname followed by first names or initials, as they appear on the manuscript)
- Title (in quotation marks) followed by "Unpublished MS" meaning "manuscript."
- Repository, or location in which it is found,
- Collection within the repository,
- Catalogue number.

White, Stanley ("Snowy"). "With "Monty" in the Desert: Reminiscences of an Infantry Corporal." Unpublished MS in private hands.

Television and Radio Programmes:

"The Collapse of the Soviet Union." Narr. Nancy Hunter-Jennings. Prod. Jeremy Parker-Smythe. *Europe Today.* BBC, Channel Four. London. (1997).

Films:

It came from the Moor. Dir. Kevin Warrilow. With Damien Roberts and Mavis Arkwright. Wrenbury Films. (1990).

Sound Recording:

Wagner, Richard. *Die Meistersinger von Nurnberg.* Cond. Stanley Oldwaite. Rotherham Philharmonic Orch. Northern Recordings. NR 8240754. (1988).

Work of Art:

Winkler, Arnold. *Lump of Coal.* Museum of Art, Chicago.

Personal Interview:

- Name of person interviewed

- "Personal interview"
- Date of interview (in brackets)

Jones, John. "Personal Interview." (27 October, 1997).

The Internet

Increasingly we are able to access information via the Internet. Moreover, more and more work is being published electronically which may never appear in print.

There is, as yet, no universally accepted method of citation of works on the Internet, consequently there is considerable variation among the style guides.

For this reason, students should print copies of material which is very important to their paper, and attach it in an appendix. In this way, examiners and teachers can confirm the accuracy of quoted, summarised, and/or paraphrased online information. Web addresses must be attached these texts. Material should be considered very important if is extensively relied upon or commented upon, or if the main argument which supports the thesis statement depends upon it.

Any Internet sources relied upon must be referred to in citations and listed in the bibliography.

The purpose of a bibliography is twofold:

- To identify the source used by a student;
- To enable subsequent researchers others to be able to find this material if they wish in order to check its contents and possibly use it themselves.

However, two special problems are faced when using Internet sources:

- Internet addresses are frequently changed, citations may lead subsequent researchers to a dead end. At present there seems no way to create a permanent citation for online resources which may be removed from the Internet, relocated, or whose content may be changed.
- Since web sites do not have page numbers, it seems impossible to direct readers to a specific point in a cited site.

The model to be followed in making Internet citations should reflect, as closely as possible, existing conventions for books and journals. Everything that appears online should be regarded as published, and sources such as computer sites, online journals and email messages, should be treated as printed matter.

Whatever the conventions adopted, bibliographical references to sources on the Internet should contain the following information:

- Author's Last Name, followed by First Name
- Date of Document (or date of last revision)
- Title of Page
- Title of Site
- Version or File Number (if available)
- Protocol
- < URL (Universal Resource Locator) or internet address>
- [menu path, if appropriate].
- Date of Access
- The author should not be confused with whoever has marked the page up in HTML (HyperText Markup Language, the metalanguage of the Web) any more than the typesetter or printer should be confused with the author of a book. Where an author is not named, then n.a. should be inserted.
- URLs are the addresses, or location, of Web pages on the Internet. The URL included in the bibliographic reference should be to the cited page, and not merely the Site.
- Long URLS in their printed form may appear spread out on more than one line. The line division should be made after one of the "/" characters, or after any of the punctuation marks.
- The date at which the page was "read" should be included in all Web citations because sites on the Web are constantly changing.
- The author's name may be found at the head of the page, at the end of the document, or following "Send comments to," "Mail to," or "Maintained by."
- Most electronic documents have titles at their head.
- The date of the document often occurs either at the head

or the end, perhaps labelled "Last revised," or "Last modified." You should always give the access date, except for email, where the access date is not required in the citation model. If you cannot find a date for the document, put n.d." in the citation.

DO NOT CONFUSE THE DATE OF THE WEB SITE OR WEB PAGE WITH THE DATE ON WHICH YOU ACCESSED IT

- The browser usually displays the current URL.
Watson, Peter, "The Historiography of the Cuban Missile Crisis." <http://www.ox.ac.uk. /history/archives/Wat-l.html> July 2005.
If the electronic work has a printed counterpart, and the printed source is conveniently available, you should use it alone and cite it in preference to the electronic source; if you used an electronic source, you should list it alone.

When you set out the bibliography, you should place sources of different types, e.g. printed sources and Internet sources, in separate sections.

Proof-Reading

The final task before handing in your final draft is proof reading – a last detailed check that all is well. Often a sentence that made perfect sense when you wrote it -- and would have continued seeming to make sense immediately afterward -- sounds awkward when you have had a chance to step back from what you have written. Small errors start to pop out at you, and you might even wonder what you were thinking when you wrote certain things. This is why you need to proof read, and why you need to do so only after taking a break.

The spell-checkers used by word processors don't substitute for proof reading. They don't pick out words which are spelled correctly but used incorrectly. So-called grammar-checkers only pick out stylistic problems in the most crude way. They fail to deal with awkward transitions, bias, unsuitable tone, and many other such problems.

- Resist the temptation simply to read over what you have written, swelling with pride as you contemplate what you have created, and then putting it to one side as perfect. That way you will not spot any errors. Pretend to be reviewing someone else's essay critically. If it is at all possible, allow a few days to pass before you do the final editing of your essay. (This is yet another reason for getting started early).

- Read what is actually on the page, not what you think is there.

- If there are types of errors you know you tend to make, double check for those.

- Read slowly. You have to fix your eyes on almost every word you have written and do it twice as long in order to proof-read accurately. You have to look at the word, not slide your glance over it.

- It helps to read out loud, because it forces you to slow down and you hear what you are reading as well as seeing it, so you are using two senses. It is often possible to hear a mistake, such as an omitted or repeated word that you have not seen.

- On a computer, spell check should be used, but this does not free the student from the obligation of checking the text himself. Spell check picks out only combinations of letters which make no sense in the language. It does not spot words which, while being perfectly acceptable in themselves, were mistakenly typed for other, similar words, and make no sense in context.

- Great care should also be exercised using the"Grammar Check." The obligation of the student to produce acceptable grammar and punctuation cannot yet be passed onto a software programme. Grammar Check is (literally) stupid, and will frequently pick out forms which are perfectly good grammar and syntax, but which are longer than the programmers thought suitable. What counts as too long a sentence depends entirely upon the context. What might be too long in an informal letter might be quite short in a philosophical treatise. The writer is responsible for what he writes. He must not allow himself to be bullied into doing something he does not feel right about by a software programme. You may want to switch off grammar check completely.

- Check more than once, perhaps concentrating on different things each time. Professional editors proof-read as many as ten times -- and errors still occur.

**IT IS NOT THE TEACHER'S JOB
TO PROOF READ YOUYR ESSAY
HE/SHE IS NOT ALLOWED TO DO IT**

Do not allow the process of editing and proof reading to go on for ever. The IB extended essay general guidelines suggest that you should do about forty hours work on preparing your extended essay. Given the marks you will get for it in the diploma, this should be considered on the generous side.

Presentation

A research paper will usually be the most substantial piece of work you will have to do during your course, and it may count a lot to your final grade. They are judged not on how much work you put in to them, or how many problems you encountered and overcame in the process of writing them, but on what you submit to the examiner. It is therefore worth taking some trouble to make a good job of presentation.

Follow any instructions given by the teacher or examiner on the presentation of the research paper precisely. Increasingly, schools and colleges will come to expect research papers to be prepared on computer. But never forget that the main goal in using a computer is not to exploit the resources of fonts and clip art you can call upon to create pretty or fancy effects, but how readable you make your paper.

The finished paper should have, each beginning on separate pages:

● Title page: include your name, your I.B. number, school, the session, subject, title and word count. (This is in addition to the official cover provided by the I.B.O..)

● Abstract
● Table of Contents
● Introduction
● main body of text
● conclusion
● Endnotes (unless footnotes or citations in the text are used)
● Bibliography
● Appendices: Necessary illustrations, such as tables or graphs, which are quite substantial are better placed in appendices at the end of the text, so as not to interrupt its flow.

Page Layout

In the absence of specific instructions, it is best to follow the following rules:

- Paper should be of standard A4 size, and of decent quality.
- Margins should be generous, at least 2 cm all around.
- Double spacing is advisable. This allows the examiner to insert remarks and comments.
- An appropriate computer font should be used, such as *Times New Roman*. Fonts designed for informal letters which imitate hand writing, or designed for graphic presentations, are not appropriate. Twelve point or eleven point would be appropriate sizes.
- On a computer, left justify the text.
- Do not split words at the end of a line.
- Do not insert spaces before punctuation marks and brackets.
- Count the title page as the first page, but do not put the number on it. Number all the others.
- Your final draft should contain no crossings-out, no marginal notes, and no hand-written insertions of any kind. There should be no torn pages, and no stains or other damage.
- Do not turn in an extended essay with loose pages. Ring binding is appropriate. If this is not possible, use a paper clip or a stapler. If you use a stapler, put one staple in the upper left corner. Do not staple the upper right corner. Do not staple along the left edge, making a "book." Do not staple along the top edge, forming a pad. If the paper contains too many pages to staple, use a binding clip or a heavy-duty stapler.
- Produce as many copies as you are required to hand in (usually three), plus one. Keep the extra copy yourself. In years to come, when your grandchildren gather about your knees and ask what you did when *you* were on the I.B., you will want to have a copy to show to them.

**WHEN THE EXTENDED ESSAY IS DONE
LET IT GO!
YOU HAVE THE EXAMINATIONS TO PREPARE FOR
THEY ARE WORTH MUCH MORE
IN TERMS OF MARKS**

Oral Examinations

Before the Examination

- Make sure that you know the material to be tested thoroughly. In order to make a good immediate oral response, you will have to have spent some time thinking about it beforehand. The better you know the material, the better you will be able to organise your thoughts into a good answer in the time available.
- Although you should be well-prepared, do not learn speeches off by heart. They will not sound spontaneous, and they will neither fool nor impress the examiner. They may not even provide answers to the questions you are actually asked.
- If the oral examination is not to be conducted in your mother tongue, then read something, or converse with a friend, in the language you will be using just before you go in to take the test. You will then be in the right "frame of mind" to continue in that language.

During the Examination

- Don't hurry. Take a deep breath, start, and continue at an even pace, slower than your normal speech.
- If you find yourself taking very shallow breaths, and getting out of breath, pause and breathe deeply.
- Pause briefly at the end of each section to give your hearers and yourself time to absorb what you have said.
- Don't mumble. Speak clearly, because the conversation is being recorded.
- Change the cadences of your voice. Don't speak in a monotonous drawl.
- Give substantial answers, which will display your knowledge and understanding, and for which you can be given some credit. Never answer with a simple "yes" or "no".

NEVER ANSWER WITH A SIMPLE "YES" OR "NO"

- Be enthusiastic.
- Concentrate primarily on getting your meaning across; not on how you appear to others or how your voice sounds.
- Take care of your timing. Don't gabble if you find yourself with too much to say. Summarise instead.
- Be accurate. If necessary, take pauses in which to think.
- Stay in focus. Do not let your mind wander.
- Don't ramble if you have too little to say.
- When you have said what you want to say: just stop.
- Make sure that your main points do not get lost in any details.
- Make sure that you answer the question you are asked, the *whole* question you are asked, and *nothing but* the question you are asked.
- If you just don't know the answer to a particular question, and cannot think of any way in which you could provide an answer for it then say so. The situation is less than ideal, but no one can be expected to know everything.

After the Examination

Like all examinations, you should draw a line under it and move on. "Afterwards" is too late to do anything about it. However, learn from your mistakes, for school oral examintions are a good preparation for college and job interviews.

The Final Written Examinations

For most I.B. students, the examinations are the most important part of the course, for the grade of your diploma. Your success or otherwise in getting to the university or college of your choice depends chiefly upon how well you perform in the written examinations. Even if you have already been offered a place at a university on the basis of your school grades, a high score might bring substantial financial benefits to you and your family in the form of college credits. These will also reduce the amount of courses you will have to take to graduate from university.

Written examinations may test:
- Knowledge of factual information;
- Understanding of ideas;
- Understanding of the application of information and concepts;
- Comprehension skills;
- Ability to analyse information;
- Ability to evaluate information;
- Powers of organisation;
- Writing skills;
- Practical skills;
- Mathematics skills
- Originality and Creativity.

As always, with I.B. examinations, the skills being tested on each component of the examination in each subject are clearly specified by the IBO, and this information is communicated to the schools. It is necessary that you make yourself aware of precisely which knowledge and which skills are being tested in the examinations which you are taking. Your subject teachers will tell you. Make sure that you do not forget, and that you are aware, during the period of preparation and the examination itself, what you have to do to score well.

You will probably find yourself feeling anxious as the examination approaches. This is perfectly normal. It is even helpful, for it enables you to decide to get started on your revision. If you allow yourself to become too anxious, however, this will interfere with your performance.

> **SOME ANXIETY BEFORE EXAMINATIONS IS NORMAL AND USEFUL**

Revision

Although international examinations are not primarily tests of memory, nevertheless some material has to be used in the examination to test our understanding – and this material has to be learned. This means that revision is necessary before the examinations. The more efficient your revision, the better your performance in the examination is likely to be.

Examinations are designed to assess the candidates' knowledge under conditions where they cannot consult books or journals. Thus it assesses the ability to organize and integrate information under pressure.

- Firstly, you have to have some knowledge to organize, and the more the better.
- Secondly, the better that the knowledge has been assimilated, the better you will be able to organize it in the examination room under the pressure of having limited time, to produce better answers.

Revision should be a continuous and cumulative process. Revise conscientiously for all your class tests and term examinations. Then you will have a good basis for your final revision.

> **REVISION SHOULD NOT BE A "ONCE AND FOR ALL" EVENT IT SHOULD BE A CUMULATIVE PROCESS GOING BACK OVER ALMOST TWO YEARS**

- Don't get worried. The more worried you get, the harder it will be to recall successfully. The key to avoid getting uptight is to start final revision in good time, aware that you begin with a sound basis.

- Start revising seriously for the final examinations at an early date. Do not leave things until it is too late to be effective. Many people pass almost instantaneously from saying that it is too early to start revising to saying that it is too late. They are simply avoiding making the effort, and deceiving themselves. Once you get started it will be easier. Revision for an examination held in May/June/July at the end of a two year course should begin during the previous Christmas vacation.

> **DO NOT LEAVE FINAL REVISION**
> **UNTIL IT IS TOO LATE.**
> **START EARLY!**

I.B. students have a special problem in that there are so many things to be completed and handed in during the months preceding the final examination (the extended essay, the Theory of Knowledge essay, various internally assessed assignments), together with other work to be done (CAS hours to be completed, the Theory of Knowledge presentation and oral examinations to be prepared for and taken, etc.). If they are put off to the last minute, you will find yourself running around completing things precisely when you should be starting serious revision for the final examinations. Under those circumstances it is likely that you will be able to do none of these things well.

Your school may help you by imposing early deadlines on these other tasks, so that you can to get them out of the way. You must observe those deadlines. They are for your own benefit.

When you begin revision for the final examinations:

- Make yourself a revision timetable so that you will give due weight to each subject. Then keep to it. Do not, however, fall into the trap of wasting a lot of time constructing over-elaborate timetables, so that you make yourself busy without actually getting any revision done. If you do this, you are just avoiding revision while fooling yourself that you are doing something directly useful.
- Apportion your time between the various subjects you will be examined on wisely. Do not spend all your time with the subjects you like (i.e. the ones you are good at) neglecting those you

have difficulty with. Spend extra time on the subjects you have problems with. Within each subject, concentrate on:

- Topics the teacher has advised that you to study especially thoroughly:
- Topics which come up frequently in past examination papers;
- Those topics you still have to master.
- Points emphasised in class or in the textbook.

Writing good examination answers is a skill and, like all skills, it improves with practice. For this reason you must use term examinations as practices for the final examination. During your final revision period you should also write some practice answers under examination conditions.

- Make sure you are acquainted with the form of the test. Some time before you take the examination you should be aware of the format of the papers; its division into sections, the type and choice of questions asked. You need to be thoroughly familiar with the layout, what it looks like, how it works, how much time you will have, and so on. None of these things should come as a surprise to you on the day of the test. The more familiar you are with the structure of the test itself, the less it will distract you on test day. You will be free to concentrate on the problems and their solutions, and not have to waste time on the directions.
- Practice. Work on past examination papers. Make brief notes, in the form of essay plans, on how you would go about answering the questions.
- Do not cut classes before the examination so that you can do your own revision at home. It is likely that the last few lessons will be particularly important. The teacher will probably revise the important topics in class, go over past examination papers, and give valuable last minute advice.

**THE LAST CLASSES ON A COURSE
ARE OFTEN THE MOST IMPORTANT
DO NOT UNDER ANY CIRCUMSTANCES CUT THEM**

- When you study during the day, you are more likely to learn faster and retain the information longer. If during your study session you feel drowsy and are about to fall asleep, give in. It is better to learn the rest of the information in the morning than trying to stay awake and forgetting everything the next day.

Revision Notes

Revision is, for many students, the most boring difficult part of the process of preparation for examinations. This is because of the way they do it. They sit with their books in front of them and hope that somehow the knowledge in print on the page will somehow seep into their brains. It will not happen. The human mind needs to be active if it is to learn. We rarely learn unless we are involved in some activity. For this reason, the student who is successful is often the one who makes revision notes (For advice on how to make them, see Chapter "Making Notes" pp.45ff).

The Approach to the Examination

The Days Before

- Make sure that you have everything you will need to take the tests. e.g. pens, pencils, straight edges, erasers, calculators, etc.
- Avoid abusing substances like alcohol and caffeine during the days leading up to an examination. There is nothing like a hangover to make you an inefficient examination candidate. Excess amounts of caffeine can lead to nervousness and forgetfulness. These are not traits that would be helpful at such a time.
- Do not revise new material the night before an examination. You want to build up your confidence by reinforcing what you know, rather than panicking yourself by discovering something you do not know. Anyway, it is too late to assimilate new material. You will need to be fresh for the examination on the next day.
- The night before the examination is a good time *finally* to go over material which had to be memorised by heart: quotations, dates, formulae, mnemonics, etc.

**IF YOU DO NOT KNOW IT
BY THE EVENING BEFORE THE EXAMINATION
YOU NEVER WILL**

- Do not go to bed much earlier than usual. If you do, you will probably not fall asleep immediately. Then you will start to think that you cannot get to sleep at all, become anxious about it, and so fall asleep later than usual.

On the Day
- Dress so that you will be comfortable, bearing in mind the likely temperature in the examination room. Dress in such a way that you can take off a layer of clothing if you get too hot. Look smart, so that you will feel confident in yourself.
- Make before you leave home that you have with you all the materials you will need. It is easy to forget something essential
- Pack a small sweet snack to provide a quick energy lift.
- Set out in good time. International examinations usually begin exactly on time. If you are late you will give yourself a handicap. Take account of the possibility of unexpected traffic hold-ups, especially in cities where these things happen.
- Do not have too much to drink before a long examination, and use the toilet facilities before entering the examination room. Remember that you cannot leave the examination room until an hour has passed, nor during the last thirty minutes. If you do have to leave the room to go to the toilet during the test, that time will not be given back to you, but will be lost.
- It is your responsibility to get yourself to the examination on time. If you arrive late, you will not be given extra time to make up the time lost.

> THE FIRST RESPONSIBILITY OF
> AN EXAMINATION CANDIDATE
> IS TO GET HIM/HERSELF
> **TO THE RIGHT PLACE**
> **AT THE RIGHT TIME**

- You should arrive early at the exam site, leaving yourself some time to calm down after getting through the traffic, and go over some basic facts or formulae in your mind.

In the Examination Room

- You must observe the rules of the examination, especially those which forbid you to introduce any unauthorised written materials into the examination room. Failure to do so may result not only in your being expelled from the examination and forfeiting your chance to take the examination; it may also result in your being barred from all future examinations held by that organisation. Similarly, and for the same reason, you must not communicate with any other student during the examination. Organisations which hold international examinations are very strict about such things.
- Listen carefully to any general instructions. Once the test begins, it is difficult to ask, and you are losing time from the test.
- Fill in your personal details on the front of the examination booklet.

The Reading Time

- Do not hold a pen in your hand during the reading time. That way, no one can think that you are writing anything.
- Read the instructions carefully. Confirm that the paper is the one you should be taking, and that layout of the paper, in sections, and the choice of questions you are offered, is what you expected. Do not simply assume that the instructions will be the same as in the past papers you have studied. If you do not answer as many questions as is required, your total mark will be less than one hundred per cent. If you do too many, the extra answers will not be counted, and you will have wasted valuable time which could have been spent on answers which will be assessed.
- Do not be shocked that the questions seem unlike any you have seen before. All students remember past papers they have seen and imagine what it would be like if their favourite questions come up. They may, but usually they do not. The chances are that the questions on the new paper you are faced with seem unfamiliar by contrast. This is simply because you are familiar with past papers, whereas this is an entirely new paper which you have never seen before. Stay calm, and you will soon come to realise that many of the familiar questions are there, but they have been expressed in unfamiliar words.

- If you have a choice, read all the questions in the sections from which you may make your choice. The choices you make at this point will probably limit the grade you can earn on the paper. you must choose wisely which questions to answer. Take up to five minutes over it, because your final mark may be significantly higher or lower, based upon how wise a choice you made.
- If you have a choice, To do this wisely, you must be aware:
    - which topics you have covered in depth in class, and which you have covered more superficially;
    - **the** topics you have the best study and revision notes on;
    - which topics you have understood best.

DON'T BE IN TOO MUCH OF A HURRY

Unbelievably, some students sometimes choose a question they know less about, and have sketchier notes on, rather than one they have fuller notes on and know more about. They claim to do this because they know they will finish the question in the time available. Having a difficulty with time is a good students problem. That is how things *should* be.

- Remember: once you have seen the examination paper, the examiner has delivered his challenge. He has done his worst. You have the rest of the time to gain as many marks as possible.

Writing The Examination

- Once the examination starts you must not be distracted by what is going on around you.
- It is easy to misread questions under pressure of the examination. Check that the question you are hoping to answer is the one you think it is, and not just the one you just hoped it would be. "Wishful thinking" in the examination room can lead you sadly astray.

ANSWER THE QUESTIONS
THE EXAMINER CHOSE TO ASK,
NOT THE ONES YOU WANTED HIM TO ASK

- Do not waste time copying out the questions.
- Do make sure that you number your answers properly – exactly as on the question paper, This can be quite complicated. E.g. "1. (b). (iv)." If you fail to number your answers, or fail to number them properly, it is not the job of the examiner who marks your script to try to work out exactly which questions your answers are intended as answers to. If you number them incorrectly, he/she will mark them as numbered.
- For each question, consider what the examiner is seeking to test. Then try to provide him with what he wants.
- Beware of questions in two parts. If you are asked to explain and to give examples, then you must do both parts to get full credit.
- You must not simply regurgitate everything that you can recall related to one or two key words in the question. Examiners call this "dumping" your notes, and they take a very dim view of it.

DO NOT 'DUMP'

- You must provide evidence for what you say. Making unsupported assertions, however true they may be, will not get very high marks. For this reason it is important to be able to cite the authors of research which you talk about; this both identifies it and also saves you from having to describe experiments in great detail.
- Keep on checking back that you are answering the question asked.
- Don't ramble. Stick to the point.
- Include as many specific references (names, dates, direct quotations) as are relevant.
- Diagrams and graphs are often very helpful because they save

a mass of words. There is no need for them to be perfectly presented; a sketch will do perfectly well.

- Few people get very high marks, and few people get very low marks, for essays. This means that the first five marks out of, say, twenty, are very easy to earn, while the last five are very difficult. If you spend extra time perfecting an essay already very good, you may gain at most one or two extra marks. But if you fail to begin your answer to the last question, even if it is an essay that you know you cannot do well, you may fail to gain the five or six you could have got for that essay quite easily. Perfecting a good essay instead of attempting to begin a last question you cannot do well is usually a bad bet.

- Budget your time so as to leave some time at the end to check over your answers thoroughly.

- You must finish the number of questions you are required to answer. If you are required to answer five questions, and all questions carry equal marks, and you only answer four, then eighty per cent of the marks is your absolute ceiling. For this reason, you must keep track of the passing of time.

- The number of marks awarded to each part of a question may be indicated on the examination paper. You must pay attention to this weighting in deciding how much time to spend on each part and how much to write. Generally speaking, if a question carries ten per cent of the marks on the paper, it should get ten per cent of the time available.

- You must not spend more time on a question than its proportion of the total mark would suggest. If you have not finished a question when this time us up, leave it and go onto the next question. You can come back to it at the end of you have time. If you go fifteen minutes over into the time allotted for the next question, you will have fifteen minutes less to complete the next question.

- Don't worry if other people seem to be writing more than you because they need extra paper. It is quality which counts, not quantity. Besides, they probably write very large letters and space their words out, or they have used illustrations.

- Do not waste time painting white-out all over your paper if you have made a mistake. Cross out unwanted material by drawing a line thorough it. The result may not be pretty, but it is the most efficient way to exclude unwanted material from your answer.

- If you find that you have left something out of an essay, insert an asterisk * at the point where you wish to make an insertion; and then at the end of the essay insert the asterisk again and write out the insertion. If you have to repeat the process for the same essay to make another insertion, repeat the process as many times as necessary, using either multiple asterisks, e.g. **, or choose other symbols to identify your insertions and the places they should be inserted in the text.
- Never save your best question to the end. Some people advise it since it would leave the examiner with a good overall impression. But the marks are awarded question by question, not at the end. You run a terrible risk that you may run out of time before you get it all down, and so spoil your best answer.
- You should never leave an examination room before time is up. You have spent nearly two years preparing for the examination. It is stupid to throw away valuable minutes by leaving early, even if you think that you have finished. You will never know what mistakes and omissions you may have found and put right if you had used the time to read over your script once more.

A Few Minutes Before the End

- Check that you have numbered your answers correctly.
- Use any spare time to check and improve what you have already written.
- Never leave the examination room before the end. There is always something that you could do to improve your grade.
- If you run out of time, then ten minutes before the end, begin to write out everything you still want to say in list or note form. That way you will at least be able to show the examiner how you would have organized your answer if you had had enough time.

YOU HAVE JUST SPENT ALMOST TWO YEARS
WORKING FOR YOUR DIPLOMA
**DO NOT RISK YOUR FINAL GRADE BY
LEAVING THE EXAMINATION ROOM
BEFORE THE END OF THE EXAMINATION**

After the Examination

Do not try to work out exactly how you did in the examination you have just completed. You will think of all the things you forgot to write, and this will create needless distress. You cannot afford the luxury of worrying about it. Forget it. Concentrate on preparing for the next paper.

Books for the IB from Anagnosis

Theory of Knowledge
The Enterprise of Knowledge 2nd ed.
by **John L. Tomkinson**
The original and most comprehensive ToK text
now thoroughly revised and updated

- comprehensive curriculum coverage
- clear explanations of logical concepts
- challenging and up-to-date examples
- detailed illustrative case studies
- ideas for student presentations
- index of concepts

Language A1
How Plays Tell Stories: Studying Drama as Literature
by **Anthony Stevens**

- practical guide to all aspects of the study of plays as literature
- emphasizes how plays are written for performance
- examples drawn from many different periods and cultures
- writing exercises help students to see drama from the
dramatist's point of view
- relates the study of drama to the Theory of Knowledge course
- extensive glossary of drama-related terms

History
Studies in Twentieth Century World History
Wars and Warfare
Single-Party States
The Cold War

- clear explanations of essential concepts
- accessible to students lacking background
- thought-provoking analyses
- subject-specific help in essay-writing
- format designed for examination revision

Chemistry
Chemistry Experiments by Marketos & Rouvas
A laboratory manual designed for IB Chemistry
The experiments are designed to:

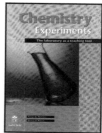

- develop the ability to record/analyse data
- comment critially upon procedures
- teach experimental techniques
- link experimental work and theory
- assist understanding of basic concepts

All Anagnosis books can be ordered online by credit card from:
www.anagnosis.gr

For up to date information about Anagnosis books
visit our website: **www.anagnosis.gr**

Anagnosis, Deliyianni 3, Maroussi 15122 Greece
fax: ++30-210-6254-089
tel.: ++30-210-6254-654